D0567002

King Arthur Today

KING ARTHUR TODAY

The
Arthurian Legend
in
English and American Literature
1901 – 1953

BY

NATHAN COMFORT STARR

University of Florida Press
GAINESVILLE
1954

TO

THE MEMORY

OF

Ida May Hill Starr

MY FIRST GUIDE

THROUGH

ARTHUR'S KINGDOM

Acknowledgments

Permission to quote copyrighted material is gratefully acknowledged to publishers as follows: B. H. Blackwell: *Camelot,* by Benjamin G. Brooks. The Bobbs-Merrill Co., Inc.: *Galahad,* by John Erskine. Brentano's: *Cesare Borgia,* by Arthur Symons. *The Listener* (British Broadcasting Corp.): "The Significance of Charles Williams," by T. S. Eliot. University of California Press: "Arthur, Dux Bellorum" (in *University of California Publications in English,* III, No. 7, 1939), by Arthur G. Brodeur. Cassell & Co.: *The Man Who Went Back,* by Warwick Deeping. The Clarendon Press: *A History of the Anglo-Saxons,* by R. H. Hodgkin; *Roman Britain and the English Settlements,* by R. G. Collingwood and J. N. L. Myres. Constable & Co.: *Scenes and Plays,* by Gordon Bottomley. Crown Publishers: *Jurgen,* by James Branch Cabell. Andrew Dakers: *Tristan,* by Hannah Closs. J. M. Dent & Sons: *Tristram,* by Frank Kendon; *Enid,* by Ernest Rhys; *Gwenevere,* by Ernest Rhys; *Isolt of Ireland,* by John Todhunter. The Dial Press: "A Bird's-Eye View of E. A. Robinson," by Amy Lowell. Edinburgh House Press: *The House of the Octopus,* by Charles Williams. Editions Poetry: *The Region of the Summer Stars,* by Charles Williams. Harcourt, Brace & Co.: *The Waste Land,* by T. S. Eliot. Harvard University Press: *Untriangulated Stars,* edited by Denham Sutcliffe. William Heffer & Sons: *Mephistopheles and the Golden Apples,* by E. R. Reynolds. William Heinemann: *Tristan and Iseult,* by Arthur Symons. Herbert Jenkins: *The Death of Arthur,* by E. S. Padmore. Alfred A. Knopf: *The Glorious Mystery,* by Arthur Machen; *Arthur Machen: A Bibliography,* by Henry Danielson; "The Great Return," by Arthur Machen; *The Secret Glory,* by Arthur Machen; *Notes and Queries,* by Arthur Machen. Macdonald & Co.: *The Bear of Britain,* by Edward Frankland. The Macmillan Co.: *Tristan and Isolt,* by John Masefield; *Minnie Maylow's Story,* by John Masefield; *In the Mill,* by John Masefield; *Badon Parchments,* by John Masefield; *Edwin Arlington Robinson,* by Hermann Hagedorn; *The Famous Tragedy of the Queen of Cornwall,* by Thomas Hardy; *That Hideous Strength,* by C. S. Lewis; *Collected Poems,* by E. A. Robinson; *Merlin,* by E. A. Robinson; *Tristram,* by E. A. Robinson. Methuen & Co.: *Pendragon,* by W. Barnard Faraday. Oxford University Press: *Three Plays,* by Charles Williams; *Taliessin Through Logres,* by Charles Williams; *Essays Presented to Charles Williams,* edited by C. S. Lewis; *Arthurian Torso,* by Charles Williams and C. S. Lewis. Pellegrini & Cudahy: *War in Heaven,* by Charles Williams; *Descent into Hell,* by Charles Williams. G. P. Putnam's Sons: *The Sword in the Stone,* by T. H. White; *The Witch in the Wood,* by T. H. White; *The Ill-Made Knight,* by T. H. White; *Arthur Pendragon of Britain,* edited by J. W. Donaldson. The Richards Press: *Odes,* by Laurence Binyon. Rider & Co.: *The Holy Grail: Its Legends and Symbolism,* by Arthur E. Waite. St. Martin's Press: *Tristram and Isoult,* by Martha Kinross. Simon & Schuster: *A Glastonbury Romance,* by John Cowper Powys; *Maiden*

ACKNOWLEDGMENTS

Castle, by John Cowper Powys. The Society of Authors: *The Madness of Merlin,* by Laurence Binyon. *Speculum:* "Arthur's Loss of Queen and Kingdom," by A. C. L. Brown. *Time and Tide:* review of *Arthurian Torso,* by Fr. Gervase Mathew. *Times Literary Supplement:* review of Hannah Closs's *Tristan.* William Sloane Associates: *Edwin Arlington Robinson,* by Emery Neff. Yale University Press: *Gawayne and the Green Knight,* by Charlton M. Lewis.

Finally, I wish to thank Professor Arthur G. Brodeur for allowing me to use material from his novel, *The Altar of the Legion* (written with Farnham Bishop); and Mrs. Edgar Lee Masters, for her permission to quote from *Songs and Satires,* by Edgar Lee Masters.

N.C.S.

Gainesville, Florida
April 16, 1954

Contents

xi

Preface

The purpose of this book is to point out the great vitality of the Arthurian tradition in British and American literature of the first half of the twentieth century. This vitality may surprise a number of readers who may have assumed that tales of medieval chivalry were out of place in the modern world. That was Walt Whitman's assumption even as early as 1871, when he wrote, in his "Song of the Exposition":

Vanished the turrets that Usk from its waters reflected,
Arthur vanished with all his knights — Merlin, Lancelot,
   Galahad, all gone, dissolved utterly like an exhalation!
Pass'd! Pass'd! for us forever pass'd, that once so mighty
   world, now void, inanimate, phantom world!
Embroider'd, dazzling, foreign world, with all its gorgeous
   legends, myths,
Its kings and castles proud, its priests and warlike lords
   and courtly dames,
Pass'd to its charnel vault, coffin'd with crown and armor
   on,
Blazon'd with Shakspere's purple page,
And dirged by Tennyson's sweet sad rhyme.

Yet in spite of Whitman's supremely confident statement, Arthur and his knights have declined to be banished; in fact they are more with us today than ever before, and have appeared even in faraway Japan. Rationalistic and pragmatic ages have a way of demanding compensations, and just as Addison's smug dismissal of Spenser was followed by a revival of interest in the *Faerie Queene*, so the twentieth century has refused to let Arthur die.

The lasting quality of the legend is not simply a result of the momentum set up by the Arthurian revival in the nineteenth century. That was a help, of course, for it gave the cycle an importance it had not had since the time of Malory. Yet the outstanding twentieth-century versions break almost completely with the Victorians — and within twenty-five years of Tennyson's death. Without question a good deal of the new creative inspiration can be attributed to the enormous vitality of Arthurian scholarship in the last fifty or seventy-five years. Vast researches, particularly in the medieval and premedieval forms of the legend, have provided fresh material which the poets and novelists have been quick to use.

One is struck by the variety and originality of the modern stories. With the Victorians the prevailing mode in Arthurian retellings was poetry, particularly the long narrative poem. The novel and the play were tried very seldom. Yet in our own day these two forms have been used again and again to very good effect. And in the field of ephemeral literature, ranging all the way from humorous short stories and poems to cartoons, comic strips, and other reminders in newspapers, the English-speaking peoples show an almost bewildering variety in their recollections of Arthur.

More striking than this variety, however, is the originality of the best contemporary stories. Here the break with the Victorians is most noticeable, in three ways: two looking to the remote past, one to the immediate present. John Masefield's *Badon Parchments* and other novels of this school create a new Arthur who is as different from Malory's or Tennyson's King as can be imagined, for he is not a medieval ruler but the British general of the sixth century, the *dux bellorum* whom the scholars have discovered in the confused records of pre-Conquest Britain. Others, chiefly Charles Williams, have returned to the past by restoring the Holy Grail to the importance it had as a Christian symbol in the legend during the Middle Ages. A third group of writers, on the other hand, reject a great deal of the past. E. A. Robinson discards the supernatural wonders of the old stories, the medieval pageantry, and the hurly-burly of knightly adventure. To all intents and purposes his characters are people of our own day, wrestling with the psychological and moral problems of a world gone wrong.

These innovations are by no means self-conscious and capricious. They are soberly conceived attempts to give new vitality to old material. The best of them succeed so well that they will probably never be forgotten. They have given fresh strength to the legend; lands but dimly seen by the Victorians have been explored and colonized.

It is true that in so doing, the modern writers have ultimately followed a pattern familiar in Arthurian retellings. They have interpreted the stories in the light of their own age. Geoffrey of Monmouth, Chrétien de Troyes, Malory, Spenser, Tennyson, Charles Williams, and Robinson: all have shadowed forth the necessities and the attitudes of their day. Future generations of critics will make the final judgment of the moderns, but this much is clear: writers of this century have often made the legend into striking tracts for the times. They believe that its lessons are for our learning generation after generation, and they have honored this belief in the vigor of their works. Arthur's Excalibur is still sharp and bright.

The profusion of twentieth-century retellings — greater than ever before in history — has sometimes made selection of material for this book difficult. In plunging through what is practically virgin timber I have tried not to lose the woods for the trees, for it is important to keep the broad lines of the legend before the reader, so as to show the way in which new versions are affected by the old tradition. Minor works are introduced for whatever merit they may have or because they emphasize the progress of the legend. I have omitted the amusing trivia which have kept Arthur before the public eye: the persistent use of Arthurian names in sports, advertisements, comic strips, etc. And I have not included folk tales — that floating body of stories, often unrecorded, which still can be found in the British Isles. My book concentrates on versions in the English language of the sort most likely to be read by those who have never forgotten Camelot.

My work has been lightened by many hands. While I was an undergraduate at Harvard, I took G. Howard Maynadier's course in the Arthurian legend and gained a new understanding of the Matter of Britain. Yet even before I went to college my mother had taken me to Camelot. To her and to Dr. Maynadier, I owe much. My wife crystallized my long interest in Arthur by suggesting that I write this book. Very shortly thereafter, President Hamilton Holt and the Trustees of Rollins College granted me a leave of absence for research in England. In London and Oxford, I received every courtesy from officials of the British Museum and the Bodleian Library. While in Oxford, I also had the good luck to meet English Arthurians: C. S. Lewis, John Masefield, and Edward Frankland. I shall always be thankful for their warm hospitality, and for the information they gave me about the legend. Fr. Gervase Mathew was also very helpful in giving me information about Charles Williams. I am also grateful for lively correspondence with T. H. White. Neither shall I forget F. J. H. Sanders and Basil Blackwell, in whose superb bookshops I found the same warm welcome and the same comradeship in learning I had known there years before.

I wish to thank officials of the New York Public Library and the libraries of Columbia University and Harvard University for letting me use many out-of-the-way Arthurian books. I am also grateful to Henry H. Wiggins of the Columbia University Press for a constructive suggestion as to the general plan of the book, and to Lewis F. Haines, Director, Henry W. Limper, and other officials of the University of Florida Press for their courteous care. Professor John J. Parry of the University of Illinois has given valuable help, not only in sending me a copy of the Northup and Parry bibliography of modern retellings but also in keeping me posted as to additional titles. To all the friends who told me of tales I had never heard of before, I send omnibus thanks, among them my colleague during a year of teaching in Japan, Professor Masato Hori of Kansai University, Osaka, who gave me copies of Natsume Soseki's Arthurian stories (*Kokyo-Shu,* 1905) and other Japanese material. I am further grateful to the various publishers who have given me permission to quote from works under their copyright. Finally, I send thanks to Professor C. A. Robertson of the University of Florida for making available timely secretarial help, and to Edith MacVeagh Huey, whose emergency assistance in typing during a summer vacation did much to put the manuscript into shape.

N.C.S.

ONE

Prelude: 1901 – 1916

After the death of Tennyson in 1892 it seemed almost as if there were nothing more that would add to Arthur's fame. The Victorians had re-enthroned him in great majesty and had even, in the *Idylls of the King,* made him the very model of the modern English gentleman. What was there left to do?

Yet how could he be ignored? The pomp of Tennyson's pageant was too strong in the mind to be easily forgotten. And his success in making Arthur a symbol of nineteenth-century ethics had reminded readers and writers that the legend could bear almost any symbolic weight succeeding ages demanded of it. For some years, however, the advance was slow. No writers of first rank came forward to rescue Arthur from Avalon. Those who dealt with him at all were mostly conscientious craftsmen, lovers of the legend, but uninspired beneficiaries of the Victorian momentum.

Even so, change was in the air, and Arthurian writers had to move with it or die. Most of them did die – to fame – but a few groped ahead and prepared the way for the revival

1

which began in 1917. Back to Malory and not Tennyson, back to the Holy Grail of the medieval romancers, and forward with the psychological realists — these were the trails that were used. The new spirit was both romantic and realistic. It was obviously romantic in re-creating the chivalric age, even when it did so in ways suggesting modern psychological attitudes. It was romantic also in its emphasis on emotion. Here one notices a definite swing away from the supremacy of Tennyson. The Arthurian people described by the writers of the recent past are more free and uninhibited than the rather inelastic characters in the *Idylls;* they are more like Arthur's Queen in Morris' *The Defence of Guenevere.* Yet they seldom venture into the dangerous extremes of romanticism; they do not approach the erotic excess found in Swinburne's *Tristram of Lyonesse.* This poem did not set the tone for subsequent versions of the story, and there is almost no suggestion of the morbid exaggerations which marked the revolutionary sensationalism of the later nineteenth century in other fields of writing. Realistically also, the Arthurian innovators knew that there were limits. There begins to be a much more searching analysis of character than before, a much more convincing treatment of emotions and motive, and a sharper observation of scene and action. One feels certain authors reaching out to find real people behind the period costumes. Yet when they treat the legend as already established they almost never write naturalistically. Sordid realism was a part of medieval life, but it very seldom finds its way into the stories old or new, save in a few of the novels describing Arthur as the *dux bellorum,* in which the old rules do not operate. In other words, the advances of psychology in the past fifty years had a great effect on the modern legend; naturalistic realism had very little.

2

The Arthurian writers from 1901 to 1916 clearly changed direction in the forms they used. The Victorians stuck rather closely to the long narrative poem. Their successors continued to use this form but they also returned to prose fiction and the drama. Since Malory's time prose had been tried very little, until Mark Twain told of his Connecticut Yankee in 1889. The drama had been tried somewhat more often, but up to the time of Wagner no Arthurian play of real literary merit had ever been staged. Hughes's *The Misfortunes of Arthur* (1587) and the pseudo-Shakespearean *The Birth of Merlin* (1662) are now forgotten by all save specialists; Dryden's *King Arthur* (1691) is a very slight piece, Arthurian in little save the name; Fielding's *Tom Thumb* (1730) is an isolated bit of foolery attached only by a thread to Camelot. Wagner's operas are among the great glories of the legend. But they stand alone; so alone that very few dared to follow him.

Unquestionably, however, the revival of the English theater in the last decades of the nineteenth century had its effect on the legend. Richard Hovey in America and J. Comyns Carr and Henry Newbolt in England had written Arthurian plays toward the end of the century. Though they were not distinguished plays, they were all serious, full-bodied pieces, and they showed clearly that writers were seeing new dramatic possibilities in Arthur. This fact is important to remember, because dramatists who revived the medieval could not help feeling that they were running against a strong pull in another direction. Following the influence of the continental dramatists, realism had become the predominant form, and has continued so down to our own day. Yet in spite of this, a large number of Arthurian plays have been written in this century, probably more than in all previous periods combined. And even though they have very seldom been acted, they are an important indication that writers are now eager to give the old stories the special emphasis of objective action dramatically conceived.

The novel has also been used to very good effect. Some of the most striking retellings of our century have been in this form, especially those after 1917 which reinterpret the Holy Grail and those which describe the career of Arthur as the sixth-century *dux bellorum*. Also, Malory begins to be treated in a somewhat different way. In spite of his indebtedness, Tennyson had serious doubts about the *Morte Darthur,* a book "Touch'd by the adulterous finger of a time / That hover'd between war and wantonness." Twentieth-century writers are not so squeamish. They began to read Malory as he is, the re-creator of Arthur's chivalric society, the whole vast bulk of it in all its virtues and all its defects. He is the "maister dere" of most twentieth-century Arthurians.

A closer reading of the *Morte Darthur* revealed fresh material not used before. *Sir Marrok,* for example, a novel published in 1902 by an American novelist, Allen French, is based on a single statement in Malory, concerning the knight who was turned into a werewolf by his wife. Originally written for boys and girls, it is still pleasant reading on a rainy afternoon, because French tells his story simply and with good pace. He knows the *Morte Darthur* and makes good use of it. King Pellinore (whose quarry, the Questing Beast, is described in Malory's terms), Tristram the great hunter, and Merlin all help the wolf Marrok fight the evil enchantment. In fact, the story has freshness and even some feeling for realism. Peasants and robbers live in the wolf's world as well as gentle folk.

Realism is carried much further in Clemence Housman's novel, *The Life of Sir Aglovale de Galis* (1905). The author (the sister of A. E. Housman) acknowledges Malory as her "most dear Master." Here again forgotten material is reworked in telling the story of Aglovale, "the worst of Pellinore's sons, the worst knight that Arthur ever made."[1] These are Miss Housman's words, however, not Malory's. Aglovale plays a very minor role in the *Morte Darthur*, being remembered chiefly for his fight with Sir Goodwin, while searching with his brother Percival for the mad Launcelot. But the mere fact that Aglovale appears in Malory is enough; on him Miss Housman hangs an entirely new story. As she describes him, he is a sorry champion; he is overthrown twenty-four times in a day. Yet though he is often horizontal, once in a while he gets to his feet and stumbles into noble action. There is all the need in the world for him to do so, not only to redeem himself but also to help preserve Arthur's crumbling kingdom. This last is the main emphasis in the novel. Miss Housman intensifies Malory's picture of creeping doom; Aglovale and the rest live in a world close to moral chaos. There is no sweet yearning for the days of chivalry in this novel. The high heroic is gone, and all the delightful supernatural wonders. Arthur's is a violent, lawless age; life is grubby and dangerous. At the root of it all is the spiritual decay in the order of knighthood, the irony of which is accented in Aglovale's curious interview with Arthur, in which he reproaches the king (yet kneeling as a penitent) for his blind sin.

Pellinore's son Aglovale had no force but to declare how the justice of God awaited Arthur to smite low his honour, and bring him as mere man to worship the law he had broken and overborne.[2]

Miss Housman is anything but a romanticist. She strips the age and its people of their glamor, for her intention is to describe what moral decay does to real men and women. In this she succeeds to some extent; her people are not symbols or abstractions. But she does not go far enough. The great central problem is Launcelot and Guinevere, yet they play little part in the story. Instead the attention is centered on the most erratic and least likable of Arthur's knights, and one soon gets tired of his roundabout, up-and-down adventures. Taken as a whole, the novel is a jumble of ill-assorted episodes. In spite of this, however, it is worth noticing, because it goes directly to Malory for new material and treats it realistically.

The respect for Malory in the early twentieth century took a different turn in several other writers. Instead of finding opportunities in the *Morte Darthur* for new invention they followed the stories exactly, and without new symbolic coloring. One would have thought that Edgar Lee Masters, the author of *Spoon River Anthology,* would use irony and realism in dealing with knights and ladies, but his Arthurian poems, "The Ballad of Launcelot and Elaine" and "The Death of Sir Launcelot," in *Songs and Satires* (1916), stick close to Malory in substance and spirit. They are so close, in fact, that they are practically exercises in archaizing. Even granting this, however, the poems read well.

"The Ballad of Launcelot and Elaine" tells the story almost exactly as found in the *Morte Darthur,* using the ballad stanza and the conventions of the type: tight narrative structure, ballad meter, repetitions, and archaisms. Yet the poem is saved from being a dull imitation by its simplicity and technical finish; a skilled craftsman made it. The stanzas describing the appearance of the Grail in King Pelles' Castle (Malory, Chapter 2, Book XI) are particularly good:

> *Anon there cometh in a dove*
> *By the window's open fold,*
> *And in her mouth was a rich censer,*
> *That shone like Ophir gold.*

And therewithal was such savor
As bloweth over sea
From a land of many colored flowers
And trees of spicery.

And therewithal was meat and drink,
And a damsel passing fair,
Betwixt her hands of tulip-white,
A golden cup did bear.

"O Jesu," said Sir Launcelot,
"What may this marvel mean?"
"That is," said Pelles, "richest thing
That any man hath seen."

"O Jesu," said Sir Launcelot,
"What may this sight avail?"
"Now wit you well," said King Pelles,
"That was the Holy Grail."[3]

"The Death of Sir Launcelot" is probably the more moving of the two ballads, largely because it is based on the collapse of a kingdom rather than on a maiden's dream. The doom of the last days, with Arthur dead and the two lovers soon to join him, is skillfully suggested. Here again Masters leans heavily on Malory. Though there are some changes of detail, the spirit and the substance of the sources are there. The final tribute to Launcelot is very close to Ector's noble eulogy in Chapter 13, Book XXI, of the *Morte Darthur:*

They laid his body in the quire
Upon a purple pall.
He was the meekest, gentlest knight
That ever ate in hall.

He was the kingliest, goodliest knight
That ever England roved,

The truest lover of sinful man
That ever woman loved.[4]

Masters should be remembered not only for the antique savor of his ballads but also for his devotion to Malory. He accepts episodes virtually as they are, and develops them in the spirit of the original. Yet this kind of respect was not enough. The strongest Arthurian writers of the century are explorative and experimental. They pay Malory the compliment not of imitation but of contemporary interpretation. Tennyson's ethical emphasis in the *Idylls of the King* may not appeal to modern readers, but he followed the only course possible to give the legend new life: he reinterpreted old material.

The most devoted Arthurian of this early period was Ernest Rhys, a prolific man of letters as editor, poet, and dramatist. Even before the turn of the century he published his edition of Malory's *Morte Darthur,* which has held a respected place for years in Everyman's Library. His three Arthurian lyrics, "King Arthur's Sleep," "The Waking of King Arthur," and "The Death of Merlin" were published in *Welsh Ballads* (1898). A few others appear in *The Leaf Burner and Other Poems* (1918); *Lays of the Round Table and Other Lyric Romances* (1905) is largely devoted to the legend. In addition he wrote three Arthurian plays: *Gwenevere* (1905), *Enid* (1908), and *The Masque of the Grail* (1908).

As might be expected, Rhys is steeped in Malory (also in the *Mabinogion* and Celtic legend generally). Sometimes, in fact, he is so under the spell of his original as to be merely imitative rather than striking out on his own. Some of the poems in *Lays of the Round Table,* for example, especially "Sir Launcelot and the Sancgreal," "The Last Sleep of Sir Launcelot," and "The Lament of Sir Ector de Maris," are

8

about as close to Malory as Masters was. Others in this volume, however, show fresh invention, among them brief excursions into the wit and irony of Dinadan and Dagonet, and the confusion wrought by Merlin's master Bleise in trying to give an account of Arthur's battles. Rhys, therefore, was not committed simply to recording the legend, and leaving it as he found it. In the Preface to *Gwenevere* (a play written for the music of Vincent Thomas) he says:

To anything like a strict antiquity, they [author and composer] need make no great claim. The power of romance is that it fits itself anew to every period. Each one takes up again the undying legend of Arthur, and more or less deludes itself into the notion that its latest version is the truest. But every century must still read its own emotion and its own colours into the past, realizing as best it may that the past and present are humanly one.

Even more important than his ingenious variations on old themes was Rhys's consistent treatment of the legend in lyric verse. His talents clearly lay in that direction; he was not a poet of high dramatic power. His concentration on this mode is a definite extension of the resources of the legend, which, up to his time, had seldom been brought within the compass of lyric poetry.

Rhys's talents are probably best shown in his plays rather than in his short poems, which are uneven in quality and give a rather fragmentary picture of the legend. Yet he could not have treated his plays as he did if he had not been a lyric poet first and foremost. In the Preface to *Gwenevere* he calls the story of Launcelot and Gwenevere "one that seems of itself to cry out for lyric treatment." He continues with a statement which helps to explain the reason for his belief. "If they [author and composer] have differed from some famous fore-runners ... who have gone to the same enchanted medieval sources, it is because their Cymric sympathies have led them perhaps a little nearer home."

Rhys's Cymric sympathy appears in practically everything he wrote; *Gwenevere* is full of it. Like so much Celtic literature it is much more a tale of mood and feeling than of action. The plot is definitely subordinated. The story itself follows a fairly familiar pattern, modified here and there by reminiscences of primitive Celtic literature. Arthur weds Gwenevere, daughter of King Gogyrvan of Caledon, whom Modred had once fought and treacherously maimed. From the first Launcelot and Gwenevere love one another; Modred and Morgan le Fay watch and plot. Finally, after a tender scene at Gwenevere's maying and an attack by Modred and his followers, we learn that Arthur has made war on Launcelot. The final act brings together Gwenevere, then in a nunnery at Amesbury, Launcelot, sick at heart and reconciled to death at Joyous Garde, and Arthur, mortally wounded by Modred at Camlan. Throughout the play Merlin is the Olympian observer and prophet, and he brings the action to a close by foretelling Arthur's immortality.

Since the play emphasizes mood rather than narrative, sharp characterization tends to be subordinated also. Arthur, in Merlin's words "He that makes himself steel / For the realm" and in Gwenevere's "a towering King / War in his brows,"[5] is not clear, even in his pathetic eagerness to give up war to regain the love of the Queen. Nor is Launcelot, save in the scene of maying. Gwenevere, however, has definite charm, because of a softness and gentleness seldom found in the story. Merlin speaks of her "frail lovely face"; her very moving has a translucent delicacy:

She steps on the darkness
With shoes white as milk,
With a shining of samite,
A rustling of silk.[6]

To the very end she has the childlike winsomeness which led her to protest, on first coming to Arthur's court, that she was too young to be Queen:

It is too soon, too soon!
The green leaves every afternoon
At home will be left wondering
Where I am, who used to sing
Against the blackbird there, and play
The leafy afternoons away![7]

This pensive lyricism — so well suited to a play with music — gives *Gwenevere* a gently appealing quality quite its own. Arthur and Launcelot and Gwenevere have validity not in the trials of kingship or the clang of arms or even in the tortured fruition of love but rather in a kind of naive and graceful inner feeling. This sensibility marks Rhys's play from beginning to end; it is this which makes action seem relatively unimportant. It is this concentration also upon the soft graces of sentiment which probably keeps *Gwenevere* from soaring into great passion. Yet there are advantages in the method. The pure distillation of feeling in Launcelot and Gwenevere somehow suggests the stylized, tapestried charm of *Aucassin and Nicolete*. The story has a kind of conscious courtliness and good taste economically achieved. One is always aware of Celtic melancholy, yet it is not Matthew Arnold's "titanic melancholy"; rather the pensiveness of bittersweet, nostalgic reflection. All in all, *Gwenevere* shows a sensitive, explorative imagination at work.

11

Rhys's *Enid* is not so moving as *Gwenevere,* probably because the original in the ancient Welsh *Mabinogion* (the source of the play) is a somewhat wry and crowded story, emphasizing, in its main conflict, a falling out of husband and wife. The larger world of a kingdom in danger, as in *Gwenevere,* is lacking. Even so, *Enid* is touched with delicate imagination and, like the earlier play, stresses romantic atmosphere rather than sharpness of character. In his prefatory remarks Rhys defends romanticism and deplores the fact that the plays of Shaw have helped to banish it from the stage.[8] This romanticism, fresh and winning, gives the play its principal charm. Geraint is its priest when he says of Enid:

> *Lady, thou hast a gleam*
> *Of stars about the hem*
> *Of thy pale loveliness.*[9]

Rhys's example possibly helped stimulate the writing of Arthurian lyrics or other brief poems, and this in itself was a service.[10] Yet lyricism is not what one usually associates with Arthurian stories. More important to the modern legend was the pronounced shift from adventure to heightened psychological tension. Before 1917 this begins to be seen in Laurence Binyon's "The Death of Tristram" and Martha Kinross' *Tristram and Isoult.* Adventure also is radically modified in the story of the Holy Grail. The old pageantry of the search for the Grail almost disappears in favor of emphasis on the supreme power of the Vessel itself as a eucharistic symbol. Though in fact this is a return to the romancers who gave a high place to the Grail in the Middle Ages, modern Arthurian writers develop the idea in a completely fresh and original way.

Ernest Rhys's Grail lyrics from *Lays of the Round Table*

and *The Masque of the Grail* are largely traditional in attitude. True, he gives the stories some originality through delicate feeling, and he makes certain changes in the narrative, not always sucessful. In the Prologue to the masque, Tradition prophesies that long after the time of the Romans the Grail will appear and become a legend; Percival, Gawain, Clamados, Launcelot, and Galahad take the chief part in the Quest; Percival resists the wiles of Nimue in the wood; as in a morality play, the questers overcome an abstraction, Timor Mortis, before arriving at Carbonek, and indeed Galahad has to defeat him a second time before entering the Castle of Pelleas ("Sir Fisherman") to achieve the Grail. These changes, however, are as nothing compared to what was to come in later writers.

It was Arthur Machen's short story, "The Great Return," first published in 1915, that gave new direction to the legend of the Grail. The author abandoned the remote past; the action takes place in his own day, at the Welsh coastal village of Llantrisant, from which come stories of strange visitations. For whatever reason, this village had been chosen to witness the return of the Holy Grail. The results are miraculous and instantaneous. As the Vessel crosses the sky in brilliant red light above the fishing boats offshore, the hearts of the fishermen are joyous; their aches and pains disappear. So in the town itself: old enmities are forgotten, a young woman in the last ravages of tuberculosis is cured, and throughout the whole of Llantrisant there is an exaltation of spirit. The divine presence, throbbing and shining in the Grail, comes to simple folk, and is revealed to the villagers assembled in the church.

Old men felt young again, eyes that had been growing dim now saw clearly, and saw a world that was like Paradise, the same world, it is true, but a world rectified and glowing, as if an inner flame shone in all things, and behind all things. . . . a world quickened and glorified and full of pleasures. Joy and wonder were on all faces; but the deepest joy and the greatest wonder were on the face of the rector. For he had heard through the veil the Greek word for "holy," three times repeated. And he, who had once been a horrified assistant at High Mass in a foreign church, recognized the perfume of incense that filled the place from end to end.[11]

With the music of heavenly bells and invisible choirs, with the ministrations of three clad in red, one ringing a silver bell, one carrying an altar top like a great jewel of blue and silver and gold, and one elevating the glowing Cup, the Mass of the Sangraal was performed in Llantrisant church.

It is hard to overemphasize what Machen set out to do.[12] It was his purpose to re-establish the Grail as a eucharistic symbol in its ancient Christian significance, and to show the possibilities of its power in the lives of people living today. On both counts he anticipates the works of Charles Williams and C. S. Lewis, who gave brilliance and strength to the most original branch of the twentieth-century legend. Machen rejects the idea of the Quest as a kind of chivalric proving ground, or as a divisive force in a "perfect" order of knighthood. He sets himself squarely against the theory that the Grail is a pagan vessel, and against the tendency to treat it as a magical cup, flitting through a fairyland. He reaffirms its spiritual essence in the majesty of a great tradition. In his later work[13] he amplifies and strengthens this conviction, as do others. Indeed when we reach Charles Williams and C. S. Lewis we find that the presences about the Grail are involved in a titanic struggle against the legions of Antichrist.[14]

In the purely human, nonsupernatural aspects of the legend, Arthurian retellings of this time stress an increasing concentration not only of the story itself but also of unleashed emotion rising from psychological conflict. This heightened feeling does not show itself in the voluptuous overflow found in Swinburne's *Tristram of Lyonesse;* it is much more like the tense, tightly packed emotion of Morris' *The Defence of Guenevere,* or the nervous, at times almost hysterical passion of Arnold's description of Tristram's death in the first two parts of "Tristram and Iseult." There was plenty of concentration of action and feeling, therefore, in the nineteenth century. As things came to be more and more in the saddle, especially with the outbreak of the First World War, this concentration was greatly increased.

A word of caution, however. Before 1917 this skillful concentration is not often found among the Arthurians. There are hints of it in Aglovale's thrashings around in Miss Housman's novel; a few other examples will be mentioned shortly. Yet for the most part the emotions of Arthur's men and women in the first years of the century are factory-made. Large numbers of stories were written, but most of them were poor stuff: lumbering, "well-made" plays like J. Comyns Carr's *Tristram and Iseult* (1906) and Louis Anspacher's *Tristan and Isolde* (1904), or dreary costume pieces by old maids of both sexes. The works that rise above this level shine bright by comparison, especially in their promise of better times to come.

Graham Hill's tragedy *Guinevere* (1906) is a little above the average. Although in spots it is clearly reminiscent of Tennyson and Swinburne, it has moments of fairly real tension and inner conflict. Guinevere says to Launcelot:

> *I fear the King,*
> *And those cold watchful eyes that never close*

Or wander from my face. I fear myself,
And thee, O thou I hold most dear, most dear,
I fear thee most of all.[15]

Hill's play suggests more recent writing in its direct poetic language and in the almost morbid intensity of urgent love, essentially "pure" even though adulterous.

Two other works of the early period, however, stand far above Hill's *Guinevere*. In fact, together with the Arthurian works of Ernest Rhys, they are the most effective retellings of their day. One is Laurence Binyon's poem, "The Death of Tristram" (in *Odes*, 1901), the other Martha Kinross' tragedy, *Tristram and Isoult* (1913).

The Tristram story continued to stand high in the twentieth century, and the honor given to it by Arnold, Wagner, and Swinburne is reflected after 1916 by Arthur Symons, John Masefield, and Edwin Arlington Robinson. Indeed, it has been the most popular branch of the legend in contemporary retellings. Without doubt one reason for this popularity has been the great success of Joseph Bédier's *Le Roman de Tristan et Iseut*. Bédier united acute scholarly knowledge of the story with literary skill. First published in 1900, his version was a translation and adaptation into modern French of medieval versions, especially those of Béroul and Thomas. By 1920 it had reached an eighty-second edition in France, and the translation into English by Hilaire Belloc has been widely read in England and America.

Binyon's ode, "The Death of Tristram," is a strong piece of work and reflects the perception which Binyon brought not only to his own poems but also to his studies of English, European, and Eastern literature. He was perhaps better known as the Keeper of Prints and Drawings of the British Museum than as a poet, but those who value well-wrought lines would do well to read him.

Like Ernest Rhys, Binyon had written Arthurian poetry even before the turn of the century. In *Lyric Poems* (1894), "Recollections of Cornwall" and "Tintagel" reflect elegiacally on the vanished glories of Lyonesse. He continues this elegiac feeling in "The Death of Tristram."

Like Arnold, Binyon concentrates on the very end of the story. Tristram lies dying in Brittany, tended by his devoted but unloved wife, Isoult of the White Hands, whom he had married after leaving Cornwall. Isoult of Ireland arrives, and the lovers catch at the moment desperately, recalling earlier events — the death of Morolt, the poisoned wound, and the trip to Ireland on Mark's behalf — clutching at the fragments of their life before they die together. Isoult of Brittany with a delicate tact has left them alone; on finding them dead at dawn she is overcome with grief and remorse. We catch the pathos of her plight: loving Tristram with all her heart, yet realizing that he was never hers. The bodies are taken back to Cornwall, where Mark ends the poem in sorrow and magnanimous forgiveness.

Binyon's poem is swift and energetic. Whereas in Rhys's *Gwenevere* time seems of little account compared to the coloring of the moment, in "The Death of Tristram" the lovers seem always to sense "Time's wingéd chariot hurrying near." This sense of urgency is carried out in the poetic form and style. The ode is written in short rhymed stanzas; the language is tough and sinewy, less reflective than impetuous.[16] And the poem is charged with tragic feeling. Love, says Isoult of Ireland, is inevitable to them; there is no escape:

> *When last we said farewell,*

17

Remember how we dreamed
Wild love to have learned to quell;
Our hearts grown wise we deemed.
Tender, parted friends
We vowed to be; but the will
Of love meant other ends.
Words fool us, Tristram, still.[17]

The whole poem is written without a trace of sentimentality. Even Isoult of Brittany, who in Arnold's "Tristram and Iseult" wrings our hearts somewhat obviously, acts with a desperate deference that much increases our respect for her. And despite compression of the story which kept Binyon from giving full roundness to his characters (King Mark especially), the tragic death of the lovers is treated with an originality and force which show genuinely independent spirit. In fact, its direct, "unpoetic" language and its reality of emotion make Binyon's poem seem more modern than its date would suggest.[18]

Martha Kinross' tragedy *Tristram and Isoult* deserves to stand high among the retellings of the period before 1917. It would probably be more impressive on the stage today than any other Arthurian play of that time.

Again the story is condensed, the action beginning well after the marriage of Mark and Isoult. Yet the narrative seems full-bodied, through three "Parts" of unhurried development. Particularly interesting is the author's successful association of Tristram with Arthur's court, as in Malory. Tristram is asked by Arthur to help him in fighting the Saxons ("Sessoynes") who have invaded Cornwall; moreover, Guinevere and Isoult are on close, sympathetic terms. Guinevere's troubled confidences at the beginning of the play about her own situation help to place Isoult's love in ironic relief and also set the tone of desperate destiny which runs throughout. Admiringly and even envyingly she calls Isoult's boldness in cleaving to Tristram

> *A wind-blown beacon shaming secret love,*
> *Our cautious smoulder eating in the dark.*[19]

The play manages to suggest the intensity of conflict among real people, rather than actors in a costume drama. This is revealed interestingly in the ironic relationship between Tristram and Isoult Blanche Mains. The fact that he had married her at her father's request and left her a virgin explains a neurotic revulsion which is not common in the legend. Tristram says of her to Isoult of Ireland, "The touch of her cold hands had chilled my heart."[20] Tristram's antipathy is powerful dramatically, because in fact Isoult Blanche Mains is not the sort of person to arouse hatred in anyone — save in a man to whom her gentle trustfulness, her hope for the small leavings of his affection, would constitute a continuous and intolerable reproach. The play is also strengthened by the picture of King Mark, who is not only the knave and coward of Malory but who seems to be torn by his own private demons. The grim scene in which he tries to throw Isoult over the parapet at Tintagil is not melodrama; it is dark psychological conflict. The play is filled with intense feeling. When Mark stabs Tristram we feel that he has taken the only way of relieving an inner situation unbearably acute. And yet above the storm of conflict one feels the presence of higher forces at work. The ocean waters seem to rise and fall about the lovers:

> *Thou art the sea at flood* [says Tristram]
> *That lifts my drifting soul against the stars.*

And at the end Isoult Blanche Mains translates the dead to another sphere:

Love such as theirs, it seems,
That God Himself doth scarcely dare to touch.[21]

The period 1901 to 1916 saw the Arthurian legend not only keeping alive but reaching out tentatively for new interpretations.[22] Malory is re-examined, lyric poetry takes on added importance, the story of the Holy Grail gains a significance it had not had since the Middle Ages, and the characters act with increased dramatic intensity through emphasis on psychological rather than primarily moral problems. Beginning in 1917 these tendencies played an increasingly important part in works which deserve to stand high in the annals of Arthur.

An Old World Newly Doomed

*"I like the romance of the commonplace — without
any guns or swords or cavaliers to speak of."*
— LETTER FROM EDWIN ARLINGTON ROBINSON
TO HARRY DE FOREST SMITH, MARCH 10, 1895.

The cool, astringent statement above foreshadows a
change of direction in Arthurian stories following the
publication of Edwin Arlington Robinson's *Merlin* in
1917. Robinson was not alone among Arthurians in his desire
to illuminate the commonplace. Though others are not so explicit as he, and though manifestoes are largely lacking, he
and his successors aimed to reconcile traditional characters
and situations with the pragmatic twentieth century. The
supernatural marvels of Malory and the romances very largely
disappear (in Robinson himself entirely); heroic adventure —
the clang of tournament and the bitter ordeal of single combat — are of far less importance than the picture, often highly
introspective and analytical, of contemporary men and women
who have strayed into the Middle Ages. In these works — in

the heroic stoicism of Robinson, the sophisticated worldliness of John Erskine, and the incisive pathos of T. H. White — we see reflections of a world shaken as never before in history. In them and in varying degrees we see reflected our own disordered time; yet we also see the basic truths of the ancient story serving as a barrier against disillusionment.[1] Probably never before had the Arthurian story been in such danger of malformation; yet by some magic the sword of Arthur was forged anew, not elegantly chased or inwrought with figures dim but nonetheless a weapon well balanced in the hand for striking at the dragons of our age — and, indeed, his also.

Edwin Arlington Robinson's profound, reflective skepticism was no sudden product of the First World War, much as that event affected his writing. Robinson is part and parcel of the New England tradition, and exhibits in his work that restraint on the surface and that passion beneath which have been so deep an influence in American life and letters. His parents were comfortably well-off folk of Gardiner, Maine; on both sides of the family his people had been New Englanders for generations. As a boy Robinson was reserved and sensitive; he was regarded as far less promising than his two older brothers. His life was rather a lonely one, yet to a very few friends he revealed a warm, perceptive nature. Of his life as a whole this is not the place to speak,[2] save to record the strength and will power with which he met a series of family misfortunes. His stamina carried him through years of neglect (or scant praise) as a poet, and even grinding privation in New York (from which he was rescued, as is well known, by a Customs House sinecure given him by President Theodore Roosevelt). After he began to be well known, the MacDowell Colony in Peterborough, New Hampshire, became in a certain sense his home. There, in increasing measure, he found the permanence and the seclusion he wished, and there he grew year after year in the estimation of American readers. Even before his death he was recognized as among the very first of contemporary American poets.

Though Robinson's cool irony and detachment would seem far removed from the picturesque excitement of the Arthurian tales, early in life he was as much taken with the legend as any young man of vigorous taste would be. At seventeen he "devoured" the *Morte Darthur,* and during his earlier years especially he showed a passion for Wagner's *Tristan und Isolde.*[3] The "romantic" and emotional strain in Robinson is often overlooked by readers who would prefer to have their authors either this or that. He fits no more easily into a pigeon-hole than Joseph Conrad or Charles Williams; as a matter of fact, in common with them he is an example of that successful fusion of romanticism and counter-romanticism through which a number of modern writers have tried to approach complete reality. Intense emotion, introspectively revealed, is at the very center of Robinson's work; yet it is emotion controlled by stoic resignation and by his insistent determination "to see things as they are." Nevertheless, to his readers he was a psychological realist, and some of them were surprised and somewhat disappointed when he turned to Camelot. Harriet Monroe, the founder and guiding spirit of the journal *Poetry,* believed that Robinson was not successful in his treatment of the Arthurian legend because of his paramount interest in the issues of contemporary life, and was glad when he came back again to his own day. Amy Lowell felt that his vision was too restricted for vital re-creation of Arthurian characters.[4] Later judgments, however, have placed *Merlin* among his very strongest poems; indeed several critics call it one of the greatest Arthurian poems of whatever age.

In the broadest sense the poem concerns the fate of a kingdom. Arthur's impotence in the face of his collapsing society is no less than Merlin's. For years the sage counselor — not in Robinson an aged man, but one just past his middle years, at the very peak of his ability — has lived in Brittany with the lady Vivian, mewed up in no hollow rock or cleft tree but bound almost as straitly by the lady's silken possessiveness. Even here in the fabulous spot that Vivian calls her Eden, Merlin hears the rumor of something like ancestral voices prophesying war. Torn by his loyalties — to Vivian who made him feel masculinely indispensable and to the King whom he had set and maintained on his throne — he turns now to Camelot and now to Broceliande. Finally the intolerable tension of Lancelot's intrigue with Guinevere and Arthur's agonized need of counsel bring him back to the court once and for all. He is done with Vivian — but too late. Tragic destiny is in the saddle, and at the end of the poem there is no escaping the prevision of doom which is to overwhelm Camelot.

From this brief summary it will be evident that Robinson has stamped the story with his own seal. It is obvious, of course, that he has transformed the Merlin-Vivian relationship from a tale of somewhat naive self-indulgence, resolved at the end through black magic, to a highly developed, credible portrayal of a man and woman who might well be living today. Robinson is little interested in narrative episodes as such. His concern lies in the "inner history"[5] rather than the re-creation of the swift and richly colored sequences of medieval romance.

Yet it is well to remember that Robinson's emphasis on "inner history" means neither that he uses the private language of much twentieth-century poetic introspection nor that he allows the world of external experience to be atomized and submerged by the chaos of the individual. True, his characters often speak or are described by indirection, yet there is never any serious doubt as to what they mean. And it is abundantly clear, moreover, that it is not the withdrawn, private Eden of Broceliande which is Robinson's ultimate concern, but rather Arthur's kingdom, gripped by a terrible doom.

Very seldom before, if indeed ever, has there been in the Arthurian story such penetrating revelation of character — of the individual who stands at the heart of the episode or the whole work. Though the attention is concentrated on Merlin and Vivian, a number of other well-known figures appear vividly, even if only for a few moments. Here and elsewhere reality is achieved often not by an objective statement of appearance or trait but rather by a kind of oblique darting at or playing about the character in an unguarded moment. It is so with Lamorak and Bedivere:

> *Sir Lamorak, the man of oak and iron,*
> *Had with him now, as a care-laden guest,*
> *Sir Bedivere, a man whom Arthur loved*
> *As he had loved no man save Lancelot.*
> *Like one whose late-flown shaft of argument*
> *Had glanced and fallen afield innocuously,*
> *He turned upon his host a sudden eye*
> *That met from Lamorak's an even shaft*
> *Of native and unused authority;*
> *And each man held the other till at length*
> *Each turned away, shutting his heavy jaws*
> *Again together, prisoning thus two tongues*
> *That might forget and might not be forgiven.*[6]

At other times the inspection is more conscious and sharp — Arthur is speaking to Merlin after his return from Broceliande:

> *"Men change in Brittany, Merlin," said the King;*
> *And even his grief had strife to freeze again*

> *A dreary smile for the transmuted seer*
> *Now robed in heavy wealth of purple silk,*
> *With frogs and foreign tassels. On his face,*
> *Too smooth now for a wizard or a sage,*
> *Lay written, for the King's remembering eyes,*
> *A pathos of a lost authority*
> *Long faded, and unconscionably gone;*
> *And on the King's heart lay a sudden cold.*[7]

In the character of Vivian, Robinson strikes out boldly on his own; she is altered out of all recognition from the somewhat petulant adventuress whom we see fleetingly in the romances. Robinson's Vivian is an extremely clever and worldly woman, and, in keeping with the author's modernism, she enslaves Merlin not by enchantment but by a kind of sophisticated fascination. In her Merlin sees the world he had never experienced, the world which he had deliberately eliminated in favor of great affairs of state. Her electric vitality catches him at a time when bit by bit the kingdom is slipping beyond his control; in Broceliande it seems well lost indeed. Very skillfully Robinson makes Vivian dangerous without destroying her ability or even her charm. For though, as she says to Merlin quite candidly, she is cruel and cold and likes snakes,

> *her beauty and her grace*
> *Made passing trash of empires, and his eyes*
> *Told hers of what a splendid emptiness*
> *Her tedious world had been without him in it.*[8]

A consummate strategist, Vivian knows the art of winning and keeping a man. Unlike certain of her predecessors she is no vulgar siren; she has no ulterior purpose in trying to enmesh Merlin, indeed there can be little doubt that in her own way she loved him deeply. She knows that an all-devouring love defeats its own end. Consequently we find her urging Merlin to keep to himself as he wishes in Broceliande, so that "Judicious distance and wise absences / [may] keep the two of us inquisitive." Even though his going is bitter disappointment to her, he leaves her Eden when he wishes; when he returns to Camelot for the last time, though fear comes to her "like a flash of a swift ugly knife," she closes the gate gently behind him.

Merlin leaves behind forever the exotic delights which Robinson describes with sudden bursts of sensuousness amid the ruminative verse. Gone are the "faint waves / Of many sweetly-stinging fragile odors," and the cherry boughs which "snowed white petals down upon him"; the fabulous feast, like one from a "devout magician's oven," is now as remote as the "half-heard, dream-weaving interludes / Of distant flutes and viols" and "Far, nostalgic hautboys blown from nowhere." That dream is fled and another takes its place in Merlin's feverish fancy — of a crimson cloud which envelops and overthrows a many-towered city.[9] Thus the extraordinarily concentrated human problem becomes merged with and transformed by the larger political one, in the light of which men and women are but the "passing trash of empires."

The men and women act out their play of vain pretension on a high plane of tragic irony. Nothing avails. The King knows of Lancelot's love for Guinevere, he knows of the danger in Modred, yet he is powerless to deal with either situation. He is like a man in a nightmare, trying to run with leaden feet. Indeed he lives in a world of haunted shadows; his nights are peopled with fears:

> *He saw giants rising in the dark,*
> *Born horribly of memories and new fears*

That in the gray-lit irony of dawn
Were partly to fade out and be forgotten;
And then there might be sleep, and for a time
There might again be peace. His head was hot
And throbbing; but the rest of him was cold,
As he lay staring hard where nothing stood,
And hearing what was not, even while he saw
And heard, like dust and thunder far away,
The coming confirmation of the words
Of him who saw so much and feared so little
Of all that was to be. No spoken doom
That ever chilled the last night of a felon
Prepared a dragging anguish more profound
And absolute than Arthur, in these hours,
Made out of darkness and of Merlin's words;
No tide that ever crashed on Lyonesse
Drove echoes inland that were lonelier
For widowed ears among the fisher-folk,
Than for the King were memories tonight
Of old illusions that were dead forever.[10]

Yet despite the acute suffering which is always near the surface of the poem, the temper is prevailingly one of stoic, ironic
calm. Like the writers of Greek tragedy, Robinson increases
the power of events by keeping brutal violence out of sight.
Even in the *concept* of violence this plan is followed. Modred,
the center of the vicious intrigue which brings about the downfall of the kingdom, never appears,[11] nor does Lancelot. We
learn of the abduction of the Queen and the accidental and
lamentable killing of Gareth and Gaheris from their brother
Gawaine. It is Robinson's deliberate refusal to make a mere
parade of events and people, arresting and even sensational
though they may be, which accounts for a great deal of his
power.

28

The ultimate power comes from Robinson's deep sense of conflict in Camelot, working itself out in agonizing, tortuous circles toward a doom which the characters, for all their vision and will, are powerless to avert. Contrary to the opinion of those critics who held that the story is really two in one, *Merlin* is a unit of intellectual and emotional design. Vivian's blandishments, playful or passionate, are not the current coin of sentimental romance, and Merlin's visits to Brittany are no casual holiday week ends but are the direct result of the insecurity, the bewilderment, and the longing for tranquillity which he shared with Arthur. Through Merlin's relations with Vivian we see prefigured the fate of the kingdom itself, for (though in a different sense) the lovers are out of the stream of time just as Arthur is. The King deludes himself that the Round Table will last forever; Merlin and Vivian believe that their passion will do so. The harrowing moment of disillusionment comes: Merlin knows that his duty lies with Arthur in Camelot; his "cold angel," Change, has put an end to the idyll in Broceliande, and Arthur is tortured by the nightmare of his disintegrating kingdom. The two stories are one; it was Merlin who set Arthur on his throne and kept him there, and who might have saved him had not Vivian been. Never, for all his wishful thinking, has Merlin left Arthur's world behind. During his days in Broceliande, Camelot has dinned at his ears, so that finally he returns, Fate-driven. There, he says, he will dig his grave, for "Time has won." And at the end he and Dagonet, the King's fool, grope their way through the night from "Merlin's Rock" above Camelot:

> *The wind was like a flying animal*
> *That beat the two of them incessantly*
> *With icy wings, and bit them as they went.*

The rock above them was an empty place
Where neither seer nor fool should view again
The stricken city. Colder blew the wind
Across the world, and on it heavier lay
The shadow and the burden of the night;
And there was darkness over Camelot.[12]

Yet it is not an impenetrable darkness which envelops Camelot. Robinson's austere puritanism is shot through with the virtues of that tough creed. "He that endures to the end shall be saved," Browning once agreed was close to the meaning of "Childe Roland to the Dark Tower Came." Something of the same sort fortifies the people in *Merlin*. Apart from their stoical endurance, not unlike that of the New England farmer wrestling with his rocky sidehill acres, there is a presence even more deeply interfused. Though Robinson was not an orthodox Christian, his work shows the compassion and the ethical authority which lie at the heart of religious faith. This ethical authority appears in *Merlin* as the Grail itself. True, in keeping with Robinson's nature the Grail is conceived more as a pure, translucent symbol of Wisdom than of Grace. It is the "nameless light that once / Had made [Merlin] see too much." Dagonet describes how the Grail came to the Round Table:

there was a Light;
And Galahad, in the Siege Perilous,
Alone of all on whom it fell, was calm;
There was a Light wherein men saw themselves
In one another as they might become —
Or so they dreamed.

. . . . . .

They all saw Something.
God knows the meaning or the end of it,
But they saw Something.[13]

The "Something" that they saw, though described in terms reminiscent of Malory, is very far removed from the Grail in the *Morte Darthur* and the medieval romances. Yet that is not the point at the moment. Those who deserve to endure — and those whom Robinson honors — are those who survive not merely by a kind of unthinking Spartan defiance of pain but by the Light which shines through all Time and endures all Change.

The dark auguries of disaster to Camelot which form the thorough bass of *Merlin* come to realization in *Lancelot* (1920). Here again Robinson had to overcome opposition. The Macmillan Company rejected the manuscript when it was first submitted, and much of it had to be rewritten. After it was published Robinson told his friend Arthur Davison Ficke that it had a "refrigerating effect on the critics."[14] In spite of early difficulties, however, *Lancelot* has made its way steadily among scholars and general readers. With *Merlin* it now stands among Robinson's very finest works. Indeed, Yvor Winters calls it "one of the few deeply impressive narrative poems written in English in more than two hundred years."[15]

In a sense *Lancelot* presented less of a problem to write than *Merlin*, chiefly because it called for less invention. Whereas almost the whole of Merlin's sojourn with Vivian in Broceliande and a great part of his association with Arthur had to be drawn out of Robinson's imagination, the Lancelot–Guinevere story lay ready to hand — and magnificently told — in Books XX and XXI of the *Morte Darthur*. Robinson follows Malory closely as his main source, though it is hardly necessary to say that he colors the story throughout with his own interpretation.

As in *Merlin*, the narrative is compressed. The action opens at Camelot, shortly before Lancelot fights his way out of the

Queen's bedchamber. The story follows the traditional pattern: Lancelot rescues Guinevere from the stake and flees with her to Joyous Gard, where Arthur (spurred on by Gawaine) follows and besieges him. After a period of inconclusive fighting, and following intercession by the Pope, Lancelot returns the Queen to Camelot and is banished to France. Still insatiate, Gawaine induces Arthur to carry the war across the Channel, but the King is recalled by the revolt of Modred. After the death of Modred and Arthur in battle, Lancelot and Guinevere (by then a nun at Almesbury) make their last farewell.

Even this condensed summary will show that though Robinson confined himself to the last part of the story, he makes a more elaborate narrative of *Lancelot* than he did of *Merlin*. The difference is worth noting, for the two poems stress complementary aspects of the same problem. Though Merlin has full insight into the consequences of his retreat he shows a certain irenic detachment; Lancelot has to face decisions and act upon them again and again. Consequently *Merlin* is a more deeply contemplative poem, in which action is not of the first importance; Lancelot, by the very nature of his commitments to the Queen, is forced to cut Gordian knots at every turn. Both as man and statesman, therefore, he is more often under danger of judgment than Merlin.

Lancelot is easily one of Robinson's greatest characters. He is a man of the intuitive tact and humane consideration not often found in the direct, forthright man of action. One senses the depth of his nature, and his surpassing gentility. This last, far more than mere good manners, is the quality Chaucer has in mind when he speaks of "Pity [that] renneth sone in gentil herte"; it is a kind of dignified, strong-sinewed compassion. This quality moves us strongly in Robinson's

Lancelot and brings him at the end of the poem to the stature of tragic heroism.

Lancelot's gentility is thrown into dramatic relief by the effect which the Grail has had on him. Though here the Holy Vessel is even less distinct than in *Merlin*, it does play its part as "the Light" by which Lancelot wishes to be guided. At the opening of the poem he has just returned from the Quest, profoundly moved by what he saw there. Although Robinson does not seem to ask us to look for God's Grace in this experience, we find again the purifying and elevating effect of ethical authority. The experience on the Quest is an important factor in Lancelot's subsequent actions. To the "gentle heart" of the knight, who could well have been as pagan as some of his fellow knights, comes a persuasion which he dares not ignore. His tolerance shows itself in his restraint with the unstable, excitable Gawaine, and a courtliness and deference in his relations with all people. Even when he has to be "cruel," in the long and harrowing scene at Joyous Gard when he tells Guinevere that she must return to Arthur, he does so as cleanly and as quickly as he can:

> *"You are free;*
> *And free, you are going home to Camelot.*
> *There is no other way than one for you,*
> *Nor is there more than one for me. We have lived,*
> *And we shall die. I thank you for my life.*
> *Forgive me if I say no more tonight."*[16]

Lancelot's desperately won balance — not often noticed because of the searing decisions he is forced to make — stands in relief against the dark confusion of Camelot. Modred is always just off stage, plotting with Colgrevance and Agravaine[17] — Modred of the "snake's brain," of whom Gawaine said: "God

made him as He made the crocodile, / To prove He was omnipotent." Terrible events are on the march; the kingdom is
collapsing, and Lancelot is sometimes gripped by dark despair.
"God" [he cries out], "what a rain of ashes falls on him / Who
sees the new and cannot leave the old!" At times he is close
to that fine line which divides hysteria from dynamic emotion,
yet he is kept from collapse by his sense of decorum, in the
highest sense of the word. He is not, as Mark Van Doren suggests, "like so many of Mr. Robinson's heroes, . . . a man para-
lyzed."[18] Though at times action is agony, act he does, and
with open eyes. He is not emotionally scattered as Arthur is
when Gawaine and Bedivere bring him news of Lancelot's
fatal assignation in Guinevere's chamber. Bedivere speaks:

> *the King is coming;*
> *Now you may hear him in the corridor,*
> *Like a sick landlord shuffling to the light*
> *For one last look-out on his mortgaged hills.*
> *But hills and valleys are not what he sees;*
> *He sees with us the fire — the sign — the law.*
> *The King that is the father of the law*
> *Is weaker than his child, except he slay it.*[19]

It is probably safe to say that never before has the collapse
of Arthur's kingdom been described with such emotional intensity. Robinson's characters, at least the principal ones, are
very sensitive instruments, tracing a long record of feeling and
resolve. It would be difficult to imagine a more highly charged
account of the relations between Lancelot and Guinevere during this climactic period of their lives than the one Robinson
gives. Guinevere is one of the most difficult of all Arthurian
ladies to make convincing, for, as Charles Williams says, all
she has to do is love. Yet in *Lancelot* one forgets that she is

usually more acted upon than acting. She is as strong as a steel spring — which is not the same thing as saying that she is violent and excitable. In scenes of long, sustained tension in the first part of the poem, when she and Lancelot grope for an answer to their dilemma and find it by cutting the Gordian knot, Guinevere reaches her conclusions and makes her points with a dialectic skill which even Lancelot cannot match. At times the steel spring lets go with startling force, as in her overwhelming anger and despair at Lancelot's announcement that she must return to Camelot. Yet she leaves, and after the final collapse of Arthur at Camlan, she who had stood between Lancelot and "the Light" sees a Light of her own, and in "calm of mind, all passion spent" gives Lancelot the only farewell consistent with their natures. In an ironic reversal of the scene at Joyous Gard, when (storms without and storms within) Lancelot released her to Arthur, she now makes the decision. The cycle of renunciation is complete — and final. Guinevere speaks:

> *"The time that we have left will soon be gone;*
> *When the bell rings, it rings for you to go,*
> *But not for me to go. It rings for me*
> *To stay — and pray. I, who have not prayed much,*
> *May as well pray now. I have not what you have*
> *To make me see, though I shall have, sometime,*
> *A new light of my own. I saw it in the Tower,*
> *When all was darkest and I may have dreamed,*
> *A light that gave to men the eyes of Time*
> *To read themselves in silence. Then it faded,*
> *And the men faded. I was there alone.*
> *I shall not have what you have, or much else —*
> *In this place. I shall see in other places*
> *What is not here. I shall not be alone.*

And I shall tell myself that you are seeing
All that I cannot see. For the time now,
What most I see is that I had no choice,
And that you came to me. How many years
Of purgatory shall I pay God for saying
This to you here?" Her words came slowly out,
And her mouth shook.

. . . . . .

A slow and hollow bell began to sound
Somewhere above them, and the world became
For Lancelot one wan face — Guinevere's face.

. . . . . .

He drew her nearer
To kiss the quivering lips that were before him
For the last time. "No, not again," she said;
"I might forget that I am not alone . . .
I shall not see you in this world again,
But I am not alone. No, . . . not alone.
We have had all there was, and you were kind —
Even when you tried so hard once to be cruel,
I knew it then . . . or now I do. Good-bye."
He crushed her cold white hands and saw them falling
Away from him like flowers into a grave.[20]

So Lancelot rides bleakly out, as Guinevere had earlier done, hearing a voice which tells him of the Light, and seeing the face of Galahad. In its tragic calm it is a deeply moving close to a drama of high obligation.[21]

It is inevitable that *Merlin* and *Lancelot* should be compared as Arthurian poems. A choice between them is very difficult, for each is conceived and executed with great skill. *Lancelot* is perhaps more sharp and exigent in its emotions, and it has of course the great advantage of the march of events (even though they are explained rather than acted) which brings Arthur's reign to an end. It is more crowded than *Merlin* with at least the implications of action. Yet to some, and I am among them, *Merlin* is a little the more moving of the two. It is so partly because of Robinson's successful invention. In the relations between Merlin and Vivian he was exploring largely uncharted ground, and in doing so he opened up areas not only of emotional subtlety but of physical beauty as well. Moreover, Merlin's plight is more dangerous than Lancelot's because he has probably surrendered more in his love. There is a great gulf between the middle-aged man lapped in amorous dalliance at Broceliande and the seer at Camelot. Lancelot, on the other hand, is a knight, one of a group whose courtly code made love even outside (or *especially* outside) the bonds of matrimony almost an obligation. Even if Christian ethics condemns Lancelot's adultery there is no getting around the fact that when he falls in love with Guinevere there is far less break with himself than in the case of Merlin. The completeness of Merlin's surrender, his pathetic desire to be loved rather than respected gives a pathos to the poem which makes it very moving. Possibly its greater reflectiveness, as revealed in Merlin's consuming doubts and fears for the kingdom (even more than for himself) helps to create a brooding sense of disaster which is a part of *Lancelot* also, but perhaps not so noticeably. Yet there is little to choose between the two.

At this point let us look at Robinson's poems in the light of the Arthurian legend as a whole. His preference for the "romance of the commonplace" profoundly affected his treatment of the old stories, and this tendency appeared also in the work of his contemporaries. His Arthurian poems show great concentration in two directions: first, in stripping the narrative down to its barest essentials, largely eliminating picturesque and extraneous adventures; second, in emphasizing internal rather than external conflict. There is very little "story" in the ordinary sense in Robinson; the old emphasis on chivalric adventure has almost completely disappeared. The "heroic" has become the stoic resolution of moral and psychic dilemmas rather than the battle against physical odds, a grim fight against disillusionment and despair. In this world of psychological struggle much that wins us in the older stories has been submerged: the somewhat artificial yet charming glorification of women, and the elaborate supernatural machinery. The Grail has been especially affected. In keeping with his austere naturalism Robinson makes it a symbol only faintly religious. It seems to typify rather a general ethical force, operating on Arthur's knights (when it operates at all) through a kind of stoical yearning for inner light, for psychic serenity.

Robinson is not the first writer who has shown these striking attitudes in the Arthurian story. They have been prefigured in a number of authors from the time of Tennyson to our own day. Yet never before had they been given such complete and effective expression.

Some students of the legend may believe that Robinson's achievements have been won at too heavy a cost. His concentration upon psychological problems has largely eliminated the elaborate pageant of medieval adventure, together with the rich and varied implausibilities of the fairy-tale sort which Andrew Lang (and a host of others) found so engaging in Malory. A number of critics have observed that Robinson's characters spend too much time talking and speculating, in a language often knotty and dialectical. Robinson also goes far toward secularizing the Holy Grail. Knowing his inheritance and training, however, it is easy to understand why he should do so. Other writers of our day have given the Grail religious significance of the sort Robinson chose not to find.

Yet though much has been taken, much abides. What Malory and others revealed of character in flashes, Robinson gives us in depth and perspective, in tales of struggle nobly conceived. Unlike some of the contemporary naturalistic novelists, moreover, he shows in his works the compassion and the ethical responsibility which have given the "Tragedy of Camelot" such strength in the past. In his poems we see one more evidence of the vitality which can survive protean changes in the body of the legend.

Protean changes, however, at least successful ones, are reserved to the few. Robinson's boldness was beyond the reach of journeyman amateurs who tried their hand at the "Tragedy of Camelot." For example, S. Fowler Wright's poems, *The Ballad of Elaine* (1926) and *The Riding of Lancelot* (1929), come close to being Victorian, and Lord Ernest Hamilton's novel *Lancelot* (1926) fails because it carries veneration for Malory to the extreme of archaized style. Capricious changes hurt the story also, especially when we learn that Lancelot loves Elaine, not Gweneviere, and in fact marries her.

The ironic, analytical temper of Robinson is largely lacking also in two works of real literary merit. Laurence Binyon's tragedy, *Arthur* (1923), though a sound and well-written play, is not particularly striking or original in its presentation. In fact, dealing more with Launcelot than Arthur, it is most successful and most in keeping with the temper of the time in its portrayal of the former, particularly early in the play, when, with the hopeless love of Elaine in his mind, he endures agonies of remorse for his sin with Guinevere. Here, and later in Arthur's forebodings of disaster, there is a heightening of emotion and an almost neurotic excitement.

John Masefield's collection, *Midsummer Night* (1928), is largely free of the frenzied, violent emotion of our day. Though taken as a whole the volume gives but a fragmentary account of the "Tragedy of Camelot"[22] it is almost continuously good reading. The reasons lie in Masefield's lively, original invention, and in his gifts as a storyteller. His happy inquisitiveness touches many a character or situation with fresh life: Morgause as a little girl watching from her covert the pirate ship of King Lot; the Saxon Loki, called "the Dragon Killer," whose raid to find the fat cattle his grandfather had reported years before led to the battle of Badon Hill; the infant Arthur taken by his mother Ygerna to the Pendragon's stone chair beside the sea to await the coming of the supernatural beings — the mailed man with flames streaming from his crown and the woman, quiet and beautiful — who will be Arthur's stay throughout his life. Masefield's imagination often touches the stories with winning surprise. Only rarely does he seem to go too far. "The Sailing of Hell Race," in which Arthur sails to America and visits the cities of Pride and Corruption, seems not only pretentious but inappropriate to the Arthurian legend. The same might be said — though it is not such an exaggerated situation — of "Arthur and His Ring." Here Arthur's dispute with Venus, Saturn, and the ancient gods over a ring he slipped on the finger of Venus' statue hardly carries the importance which Masefield probably wished to give it. Yet if in one or two cases his imagination runs away with him, for the most part his collection does well by the legend. And it goes without saying that in scenes of action and in the combination of the picturesque and active Masefield is very successful. "The Taking of Morgause" might stand as a model for the treatment of a new episode. Delicate in its picture of the hidden, watching little girl, swift and clear without brutality in its account of her abduction, it is difficult to see how it could have been done better. In scenes of struggle like "Badon Hill," and the sequence describing Lancelot's discovery in Gwenivere's chamber, in "The Fight at Camlan" and "The Fight on the Beach, or the Passing" the clang of conflict is pictured with Masefield's skillful handling of detail and narrative movement. Finally, as a point of slight connection with Robinson, while he does not eliminate the supernatural, as Robinson does, he depends on a rather simple and realistic interpretation of events. The story of the death of Arthur, for example ("The Fight on the Beach, or the Passing"), emphasizes more the savage, brutal combat on the seashore than the wonderful and the strange. Excalibur is not returned to the mere at all, and even though a ship comes with Arthur's "Helper" and seven Queens to take him to Avalon, this conclusion is touched lightly. It is the terrible struggle by the sea which stays in the mind, rather than the manner of Arthur's translation.

While Binyon and Masefield occupy a place roughly between the old and the new, a number of other contemporary writers are clearly children of the restless, disillusioned, and "realistic" twentieth century. *Camelot,* a little-known poem by Benjamin Gilbert Brooks, published at Oxford in 1919, is interesting for the titanic confusion and despair which the author transferred from his own world, exhausted by the First World War, to Arthur's kingdom. *Camelot* is a confused and confusing mélange, an impressionistic picture of evil and disaster in which Guenivere is represented as an oriental princess in a lush, exotic setting. Gawaine kills her with his mace because of her affair with Launcelot. In the last scene Modred finds Arthur dreaming on his throne amid clouds of perfume and "gorgeous Persian stuffs." He reproaches the King with the lust and evil of the kingdom and Arthur kills him. It is a nightmare land. Launcelot seeks the Grail through "dry curst ground" and a "beer-coloured world." And the questing Galahad, after being smitten by an angel with a flaming sword, finds himself in

> *an elvish world, where he saw rise*
> *'Mid cloudy phantom-whorls, vast forms that strode*
> *All dumbly through the gloom, till spectral foes*
> *Entangling, slew them. Aeons he abode*
> *To learn the truth thereof.*[23]

Brooks's poem therefore suggests the overwhelming evil which later authors have shown looming over the land of Logres. And while it is an erratic picture of Camelot, its point of view, as well as its somewhat cryptic and allusive manner, stamp it as new writing rather than old.

A final group of works, all but one of them novels, is marked in one way or another with the skepticism, "realism," and worldliness which characterize the Arthurian poems of Robinson. Even so, however, the difference is considerable, for in most of them we find a kind of shallow cynicism, or a brittle, drawing-room sophistication which is far from the searching melancholy of *Merlin* and *Lancelot*. Chester Keith's *Queen's Knight* (1920), unfortunately subtitled "A Prose Epic," is a long, conscientious, and uninspired novel about Lancelot and Guinevere, running from Lancelot's youth in Benoic to the death of the lovers. A stuttering redaction of Malory with a dash of Tennyson, it does make one or two concessions to the new spirit. Its aim is to deal with "real" people. "Into the bourneless country and dateless period of romance" — Keith says in the Preface — "I have endeavoured to transport ordinary human beings." Even more to the point is a strong touch of worldliness in the young Lancelot, who early advises his cousin Bors never to get mixed up with women. The anti-romantic hints in *Queen's Knight* are given full body in Philip Lindsay's novel *The Little Wench* (1935), again a detailed account of Lancelot and Guinevere (the "wench" of the title). Realism is carried to the point of brutality. Arthur's standing army are rascals who "delighted in murder, rape and every sin." Lancelot seduces Elaine le Blank while drunk, and when his son Galahad is serving as his page years later, he beats him savagely.[24] Love is often described with contempt; Merlin calls it "God's trick to produce children" and Dinadan refers to lovers as "life's lepers, spreading a disease that no chirurgeon but the knife can cure," and often in the book the female form is thrust at the reader. As Lindsay truly says in his Dedication, "the men are violent, the women obsessed by sex," a point of view which tends to distort his realistic intention to change Arthur and Galahad "from symbolism to humanity." Lindsay's defiant "modernity" of tone and his sensationalism obscure strong, well-written passages. The picture of Galahad — dark, tense, and fanatic — while very far from the usual idea, has a certain power; and the scene of Merlin's revelation of his secrets to Nimue calls up a picture of diabolism not too far removed from what Charles Williams had done five years before in *War in Heaven*. Lindsay shows care also in describing medieval social functions and dress.

John Erskine's *Galahad* (1926) is the best-known of the worldly-wise, sophisticated Arthurian stories.[25] While it does not equal T. H. White's *The Ill-Made Knight* as a serious tale, it is free from the crudities of *The Little Wench*. Erskine's skeptical attitude is clear from the very outset. He has no intention of perpetuating fanciful legends about Pelles, Lancelot, and Elaine, but rather, he says we shall tell the story as it happened in our world, to people like ourselves or only a little better — the story, that is, as it was before poets lifted it out of its origin and used it as a language for remote and mystical things. . . . We say nothing here of the Grail, nor of Joseph of Arimathea, nor of the Round Table, nor of Excalibur.[26]

With this purpose he deals with the triangle, Lancelot, Elaine, and Guinevere, carrying the tale from the conception of Galahad (in which, of course, enchantment plays no part) to Lancelot's retreat to the holy life. Needless to say, it is a story in which chivalry comes in for rather rough treatment. Elaine protests that tournaments are out-of-date, and that jousting is "murder," and Guinevere is a complete skeptic on the subject of trial by combat:

I suspect the strongest arm wins, and the freshest horse, and the keenest eye — and the greatest skill and experience. Innocence and virtue have nothing to do with it.[27]

The Grail fares far worse even than in Robinson. Although at the end of the book Brother Martin, Lancelot's confessor, tells him that Galahad is searching for "the holiest treasure in the world" we can doubt that he would ever find it, because he is anything but spiritual. Guinevere was probably to blame. Like Hedda Gabler, she was a devastatingly energetic modern woman with a yearning to mould human destiny ("To be happy," Lancelot says to her, "you need a man around to make something out of"); not doing so well with Lancelot she turned to his son, who, she tells Lancelot, is to be her master-piece — spiritually strong and physically clean. The strength behind a singularly sterile morality is evident in a Galahad who becomes priggishly outraged when he learns of his father's goings on with Elaine and Guinevere. The spiritual side of the Arthurian story has undergone many a sea change and many a sad falling-off in the long history of the legend; probably it has taken few strokes so dolorous as this degradation of the Galahad who in Malory begged his companions to commend him to his father Launcelot before going to the Holy City of Sarras.

The more's the pity, for Erskine shows in the first half of his story that he has some understanding of the pathos and tension within the triangle. As the story goes on, it bogs down in tiresome talky-talk. The superficial glitter of the smart drawing-room conversation (the characters talk interminably!) palls quickly, and Guinevere becomes more and more boring. Lancelot's long devotion to this bossy, possessive, and unpredictable female in preference to Elaine is difficult to understand. Perhaps it can be explained only in the light of a remark he makes to Pelles: "My habits are of the most active kind. Ordinarily I'm not what you'd call a thinking man."[28]

Erskine's *Galahad* falls between the two stools of extravagant satire and serious narrative. His desire to re-create the story in the modern, sophisticated, "realistic" idiom prevents him from achieving the one; his uncertainty in characterization and his artificial raillery stop him short of the other.[29]

Up to this point the modern spirit has not served the Arthurian novel very well. With the publication in 1940 of T. H. White's *The Ill-Made Knight*, however, the situation is changed. White was already well known as the author of *The Sword in the Stone*, a brilliantly amusing — and serious — improvisation on the boyhood of King Arthur, and *The Witch in the Wood*, a farcical account of Morgause of Orkney. In *The Ill-Made Knight* he writes soberly (or as soberly as he can) of Launcelot, Guinevere, and Elaine. It is a genuinely moving account.

45

White's serious study of the Arthurian legend, as described in Chapter V, confirmed him in his love of the early stories. These he touches with brilliant invention quite of his time and quite his own. His great master is Malory (in whom Launcelot was the "Chevalier Mal-Fet"); throughout *The Ill-Made Knight* we find the substance and even the very language of the *Morte Darthur*. Yet he writes with such a modern attitude toward character and such effortless learning that his book is refreshingly original.

The Ill-Made Knight is of much greater range than the other novels of this group. This superiority does not depend on White's extending the story to cover a long period, for others have covered as wide a span as he, but rather on his understanding of the forces which made tragedy inevitable. The problem which faces Lancelot is knit together with the problem of the whole kingdom; the one illuminates the other. White's treatment of situations which Malory touches only lightly is skillful indeed. From the first, when Arthur invites the young Lancelot to join him in fighting against Might, it is clear that great issues are at stake. White has his eye on the kingdom, for Arthur is beset with vexing problems of leadership to the very end. There was the quarrel with the "tory barons," for example, early in the reign — those disaffected Kings in Malory who had to be overcome before Arthur could feel secure as a King. After he has subdued these crusty conservatives, these writers to the *Times,* as White puts it, in a "civil war of ideologies," there arise the new difficulties of peace. The Round Table and the Quests, instituted to further a noble chivalric end, often had the opposite effect. "Civilization" turned into "sportsmanship," and the knights set great store by their tilting averages. All of this leads to more sinister things: the feud between the families of Pellinore and Lot;

the wholesale disaster, physical and spiritual, which the Grail Quest brings, especially as seen in Gawaine's callous account of his brutal battles; and finally the dry rot at the heart of courtly love in Tristram and Lancelot. All this Arthur sees quite clearly. Even before the Quest for the Grail is instituted he speaks bitterly to Lancelot: "Don't ever let anybody teach you to think, Lance: it is the curse of the world." Now that Right is established, he continues, there is nothing left to fight for, yet the fighting still goes on. The decay begun with "Games-mania" had continued with murder. The only salvation in checking "open manslaughter" and "bold bawdry" would be spiritual faith.[30] The bitter irony of the situation is clear: Arthur's court has decayed because of, or at least simultaneously with, the establishment of Right by force. The King created a perfect order — and found it rotten at the core!

The world White describes is varied and alive. The author projects himself into the Middle Ages with complete ease. He is so clearly an expert in the field that when he describes the interior of the armory in which the young Lancelot got his first knightly training from that amazing old instructor, Uncle Dap, we gain an accurate idea of the mechanics of knighthood. White wears his learning easily; his description of Lancelot's arming himself for his departure from Elaine's castle is a model of what such a passage should be, sharp in detail, and economically written.

There is a good deal of satiric wit in the book, and this presents a problem. In *The Sword in the Stone* White's imagination leaps in hilarious bounds, and we are glad that it does, for in a world of boyhood wonders anything can happen, even the appearance of medieval characters who talk like the people in *Punch*. Merlyn, who lives both forward and backward in time, sets the stage for extravagant marvels of magic — and anachronism. The world of *The Ill-Made Knight,* however, is a much more sober one; indeed the story has the makings of tragedy. Some of the comic relief is good — eccentric Uncle Dap, for example, and the bumbling, genealogical King Pelles — because these figures are conceivably of their time. When White uses out-and-out anachronism, however, in mentioning the "tory barons" who are writers to the *Times* and in describing Sir Turquine's prison as "a sort of concentration camp," one feels that the author should make up his mind what kind of story he wants to tell. The abduction of Guenever by the cockney knight Sir Meliagrance is a case in point. Taken by itself it is a very funny story, but it seems definitely out of key with the pathos and tension built up through Lancelot's battle as the Queen's champion against Sir Mador, and the suicide of Elaine.

It is true, however, that comedy for its own sake plays a far less important part in *The Ill-Made Knight* than in White's other Arthurian novels. In fact the story is a serious and moving one. Near the close, the author says of it: "It is a story of love in the old days, when adults loved faithfully: not a story of the present, in which adolescents pursue the brief and ignoble spasms of the cinematograph."[31]

It is indeed a story of love of the old kind, and a poignant account of Lancelot's ill-starred private life. Elaine emerges vividly; a pretty girl but dull, growing a little dumpy during the course of the years, and more and more pathetic in her yearning for the happiness she had had for a few brief moments. Her suicide (a fusing of the two Elaines) intensifies the irony of Lancelot's situation toward the close of the book. Guenevere is also quite a likable woman. During most of the story she manages to be intense without being either vixenish or worldly-wise (as in Erskine); even in her stormy scene with Lancelot after she discovers the affair with Elaine she is not only convincing but somehow appealing. As time goes on the irony of circumstance grips her as it does Elaine, and even Lancelot himself. Her own satisfaction seems hardly worth the winning in the face of the gradual decay of all that Arthur prizes. The tragedy of being childless, the tragedy of Lancelot's divided loyalties, reduces her to a kind of tolerant passivity, and we see her at the end of the book in a mood of autumnal calm, no longer possessive of her lover, content to let him cleave to the God he sought. White develops Lancelot himself with strength and originality, and skillfully emphasizes the pathos of his situation. This is not a story which carries the fortunes of Arthur, Lancelot, and Guenever to the bloody field of Camlan and the death of the lovers in the odor of sanctity. White stops short of the high heroic; the tale comes to a gentle end with the lovers resigned to what they must be. Yet in a sense there is a resolution for Lancelot. All his life he had felt insecure; something was wrong with him. "Lancelot was not romantic and debonair," says the author; what he regarded as his ugliness made him think of himself as "the ill-made knight." A feeling of inferiority — so little warranted in actual fact — constantly drove him to make himself pre-eminent at Arthur's court. Yet when he had done so, there fell the shadow. His irresistible attractiveness to women, even his greatness as a fighter became of little worth to him in the face of his active conscience. The world of Camelot was falling around him and he seemed powerless to avert the final collapse. In typically skeptical fashion White even denies him much satisfaction from the Grail or his son Galahad, who as a boy was more interested in playing with dolls than with toy knights. Yet Lancelot seeks God, and he passionately desires some sign of Divine Grace. At the very end it comes to him.

49

He recaptures his faith by miraculously curing the wounds of the Hungarian knight, Sir Urre. So the story comes to a close with a kind of gentleness. Guenever has accepted her fate and Lancelot has saved something from the ruins of Camelot.

If *The Ill-Made Knight* is not heroic tragedy at least it is very real pathos. White reveals the tensions and inner conflicts of characters moving through a doomed world. Here, as in Robinson, the virtues of the book outweigh the concessions the author makes to modern taste. Though the Grail is much subordinated, a miracle can still occur; Lancelot's faith is spectacularly vindicated. And though the actors speak like people whom we might know, they speak like the most interesting and not the most trifling of our friends. Finally, *The Ill-Made Knight* wins us because the author knows the meaning of that abused term, prose style.

The world-weariness of the twentieth century, therefore, failed to injure the "Tragedy of Camelot." On the contrary, in the poems of Robinson and in White's novel, we see the familiar story taking on new strength.

THREE

The Tragedy of Cornwall

T he legend of Tristram and Isolt has held a very important place since 1917. Playwrights, poets, and novelists have told the story as often as in the period just preceding and they have told it much better. The versions of John Masefield, Thomas Hardy, Arthur Symons, and E. A. Robinson deserve a high position in the history of the legend.

Though in general there has been less tendency to invent new material in this tale than in other branches of the cycle, the restless, inquisitive spirit of the last three decades has left its mark. The story remains much as it had been before, but in the best versions it is apt to be much condensed and to rely on analysis of motive, and to emphasize feeling at times almost neurotic. The skepticism, sophistication, and "realism" of a modern world out of joint play a strong part. In fact, even though versions in the new mode are outnumbered by traditional retellings,[1] new wine has been poured into old bottles with marked success.

The year 1917 was a good one for the Arthurian legend. Robinson's *Merlin* interpreted the tale of Vivian and her assotted sage in terms meaningful to an unsettled time, and Arthur Symons revealed in his play *Tristan and Iseult* the almost hysterical compulsiveness of the modern temper. How much of this feeling can be laid to Symons' fervor as one of the rear guard in *fin-de-siècle* attitudes and to the nervous instability which led to his temporary mental collapse it is difficult to say. Whatever the reason, his *Tristan and Iseult* has an urgency which makes it not only very much of his time but also one of the two or three most compelling versions of the story in our day.

Though Symons' version follows the standard pattern of action from the time when Tristan comes to the Irish court seeking the hand of Iseult for his King down to his death from Meriadoc's poisoned dagger, the story gives the impression of being compressed and simplified. This can probably be explained by the clean line of action throughout and by motivation which is clear and strong. It is as if a single wire, bright and naked of insulation, carried a current of great force.

In the first act Tristan comes to the Irish court to ask the hand of Iseult for King Mark. There he finds Iseult's two cousins, Iseult of Brittany, who quietly falls in love with him, and Meriadoc (who, as in Thomas, loves Iseult of Ireland) sworn to avenge the death of his father, Morolt. Apparently there is no early love between Tristan and Iseult; indeed when she discovers (through the missing fragment in the sword) that he had slain her uncle, she is prevented from killing him outright only by Iseult of Brittany and the Queen. (In Thomas and Gottfried von Strassburg it is the Queen who wishes to kill Tristan.) Finally, under the laws of hospitality the visitor is protected, and the marriage to Mark is arranged.

The second act takes place on board ship. Iseult is disturbed; she has no heart for the marriage, and the death of

Morolt rankles. Yet she sees no point in carrying the feud further and persuades Meriadoc to swear that he will not harm Tristan. Then she calls for wine, that she may seal a peaceful agreement with her uncle's slayer. As in Gottfried von Strassburg, a little child mistakenly brings the love potion. Love sweeps over them as the ship nears the coast of Cornwall.

Following the Wagnerian arrangement of scenes already established in Act II and to be continued in Act IV, Act III is set in King Mark's garden. Melot, the King's fool, tells Mark of the lovers' meetings, only to be met with shocked disbelief. Finally, however, the King consents to return early from a hunt to resolve his doubts. The action moves to the lovers in the garden, caught in the net of their dangerous situation. Tristan, distraught by his obligation to the King, feels that he must leave; Iseult is more passionately daring. At this point they are surprised by Mark, Melot, and the royal followers. The King rebukes and upbraids Tristan, who, as in Wagner, shows every sign of repentance. Iseult, on the other hand, defends her love. The act closes with the banishment of Tristan.

Act IV finds Tristan in Brittany, mortally wounded by Meriadoc's poisoned dagger, and tended by Iseult of Brittany, whom he had married after setting her father's dukedom to rights. To the torture of his gentle wife, his sole hope rests in the arrival of Iseult of Ireland before his death. Finally there comes the familiar episode: Iseult of Brittany tells him that the approaching ship carries a black sail. As in Thomas, he dies before the reunion. Iseult enters to find her lover dead, and she herself dies. Mark speaks the final words.

The strength of the story lies largely in the figure of Iseult, who is much more expressive and vigorous than Tristan. In her (and others in the modern story like her) we see the lady's supremacy under the code of courtly love reinterpreted as nervously urgent possessiveness or even ruthlessness,[2] perhaps the corollary of the freedom the "modern woman" has newly won. Her raptures, to paraphrase Drayton's lines on Marlowe, are all light and fire. Yet there is the dark consequence: light blinds and fire burns. After she drinks the love potion Iseult speaks in words filled with dark suggestion:

> *I feel*
> *As if a boundless joy had given me wings:*
> *I am as universal as the sun.*
> *Look, Tristan, there is nothing here but light:*
> *Light in the sky, light in the hollow sea,*
> *The encircling and caressing light of the air!*
> *Light eats into my flesh and drinks me up:*
> *I am a cup for the immense thirst of light;*
> *I cannot see you, Tristan, for the light.*

After the ecstasy of the moment passes she is a prey to fears:

> *I am afraid, I am afraid of love.*
> *This is some death that has got hold on me;*
> *The night is coming back into my soul.*[3]

Her love for Tristan is like a flame that ultimately consumes its kindlers. "Love is a fire," she says, "and burns all lesser things," the same fire she would be so as to burn Tristan's lips. Yet the fire consumes itself. Iseult looks upon the dead body of Tristan:

> *This dust was once a fire and burned the stars:*
> *Now what a little ashes holds the fire*
> *That was blown out too early. There is nothing*
> *Left in the world, and I am out of place.*[4]

The play is really Iseult's in the sense that it is she who daringly projects her love.[5] Tristan seems like a man at times almost overborne by the intensity of her passion, the prey of dark questionings. In fact, the weakness of Symons' play, not unlike Robinson's *Tristram*, would seem to be that Tristan is a defeated victim of love rather than a passionate sharer in it. His honor always rises to haunt him:

> *Love is not love* [he tells Iseult] *unless it honour honour*
> *Above all mortal things.*

At this point, long before his death, he realizes what he has lost and despairingly leaves his fate in Iseult's hands:

> *The world passes away,*
> *You have put the world into a dusty pit,*
> *And all is covered up. Do with my life*
> *What you would do with it.*[6]

He dies almost as a sacrificial victim, even deprived of the solace of seeing Iseult before he expires, brought low in the shadow of pathos rather than high tragedy.

Yet it is perhaps too much to expect that the passion which Symons pours out so prodigally in Iseult should be equally intense in Tristan. Her lavishness of feeling needs must serve them both. By and large it does, for while the energy which went into the all-consuming Iseult leaves Tristan somewhat drained, while it reduces the importance of Mark, it raises Iseult to a high level of tragic passion. It even seems to affect the usually meek and self-effacing Iseult of Brittany by contagion.[7] As she watches the dying Tristan she breaks out angrily against the cruel turn which compels the wife to acquiesce in the rival's coming:

> O
> *The bitterness of love, the hate of love,*
> *So kind in the beginning and so sharp*
> *A sickle when the seed has come to ear!*[8]

Indeed it is the bitterness of love, love which is "more cruel than a savage beast," as Iseult's mother tells her early in the play, which hovers constantly above the surface of passion.

Symons' sense of the bitterness of love rather than its high exaltation, as well as his stripped and sinewy style mark his play as characteristically modern.[9] The pangs of tragedy become altered into something like frustration and disillusionment; the "grand manner" of oratory and dramatic emphases — with all that this method implies at its best and worst of majestic feeling or mere artifice — has given way to neurotic excitement, to the compulsive drives of intense psychological conflicts. The end of the play, one feels, brings the lovers to a truce of exhaustion, not unlike the uneasy respites which a confused world has snatched from violence in the last four decades.

Yet it would be a mistake to assume from Symons' play published in the year of America's entrance into World War I that the insecurity of the new age was to color all subsequent retellings of the Tristram story. Well over half of the versions published after 1917 either bear no unmistakable marks of the modern temper or definitely suggest the manner of the previous fifty years. True, the novels of John Erskine, Mary Ellen Chase, and Hannah Closs, and Robinson's poem *Tristram,* are unmistakably modern in tone. Yet there is no unanimity, rather wide variety in the approach to the "Tragedy of Cornwall." D. M. Mitchell's tragedy *Sir Tristram* (1929), for example, is written in Tennysonian blank verse of a heavy, sprawling kind. Ernest Reynolds' poem *Tristram and Iseult* (1930), described in the prefatory note as "idyllic fantasy" and "pictorial poetry" rather than narrative, is a strange mélange of Wagner, Swinburne, and the Pre-Raphaelites, with occasional touches of wry modern imagery. An Philibin's *Tristram and Iseult* (1924) derives whatever faint charm it may have as a poem from a childlike Iseult who suggests the naive Gwenevere of Ernest Rhys's earlier play. Still derivative in manner but superior to the others in this group is Frank Kendon's narrative poem *Tristram* (1934). Its chief virtue lies in its directness and compression, though this last has disadvantages in a brief work which treats the story from Tristram's bringing Iseult to Cornwall down to his death. It is so short, in fact, that the characters are not clear; Mark, for example, is hardly seen at all. Its virtue, however, lies in its underwritten simplicity — the passion of the lovers is suggested more often than stated — and in a lyric and elegiac tone throughout. The author shows a loving eye for nature more to be expected in a Victorian than a modern poet, and the sections of the poem are interrupted by lyrics of Tristram's own singing, several of which are quite graceful. Though it is an unpretentious poem — perhaps *because* it is unpretentious — Kendon's *Tristram* deserves a modest place in the history of the legend. We may take leave of it with Iseult of Brittany watching over the dead lovers:

> *Look, widow lady, where they lie;*
> *All lovers are but he and she . . .*
> *Lasting silence filled her soul . . .*
> *Brightness over-ran the sea. . . .*

Somewhat more modern in feeling, though it does not equal Symons in this respect, is John Todhunter's play, *Isolt of Ireland* (1927). Todhunter's heroine is a wild and stormy Isolt; her passion is poured out quite as easily as in Symons' play. Yet Todhunter seems to suggest Celtic emotionalism rather than neurotic disbalance. And there is in Tristram's words to her something of the conventionally "poetic" and decorative attitude toward strong feeling:

The wildness of the winds is in thy words,
My ocean child, and the salt ocean wind
Has revelled in thy hair. The sea, the sea!
There sounds the note of danger, which thy sight
Had lulled to sleep with old forgotten things.[10]

Isolt's plea to her lover is even more forced and flat:

Oh my life's lord!
My breast is earth waiting the touch of spring;
Comfort its cold, for I am sick with longing.
But now, no time for solace of sweet words,
Each moment is a traitor. Oh, my love,
We must fly, fly to-night![11]

Yet though faults of expression, structure, and characterization weaken Todhunter's play, it has moments of rough vitality. The picture of an ambivalent Isolt — hating Tristram as well as loving him — is appropriate to an age which has allied psychiatry and literature, and the Prologue, by far the best part of the play, conveys some of the wildness which animated both the sea and the lovers on their trip from Ireland to Cornwall.

In 1923 Thomas Hardy surprised many of his readers by publishing an Arthurian play: *The Famous Tragedy of the Queen of Cornwall.* Long before, he may have been moved by the Tristram story, if we can believe the implications of his poem "When I Set Out for Lyonnesse," written as early as 1870. Though it makes no mention of the legend, it does suggest the fascination of ancient mystery and magic, especially in the second stanza:

What would bechance at Lyonnesse
While I should sojourn there
No prophet durst declare,
Nor did the wisest wizard guess

What would bechance at Lyonnesse
While I should sojourn there.

In the third and final stanza Hardy returns from Lyonnesse
"With magic in [his] eyes."

The magic that he may have felt long before, however, is
not present in the *Famous Tragedy;* at least it is not the naive
devotion to love and the miraculous wonders of the medieval
romances that we find there. The play is conceived in a lofty,
objective, and almost classical mood. Fate characteristically
hovers overhead; the characters would probably be quite at
home in Hardy's Wessex.

The title page describes the play as "A new version of an
old story arranged as a play for mummers in one act requiring
no theatre or scenery." In brief compass it tells the tale of
Tristram's death. Iseult in Cornwall has heard that Tristram
lies ill in Brittany and takes ship. The familiar legend of the
black and white sails plays its part: when the whitehanded
Iseult falsely tells Tristram that the sail is black he has a
relapse, and when the ship docks, Iseult is told that her lover
is dead. She returns to Cornwall. Meanwhile Tristram has not
died. Enraged by his wife's deceit, he sails for the court of
Mark disguised as a harper. Eventually his disguise is pierced
by the treacherous Andret and (as in Malory) he is slain by
Mark, who in turn is killed by Iseult. She then joins her lover
in death by leaping from a cliff with her dog Hodain, and
Iseult of Brittany, who has come to Cornwall seeking Tristram,
is left to mourn the multiple disaster.

Hardy's play emphasizes the inevitable march of doom
rather than the relationship of the principal characters, especially as seen in the passionate oneness of the lovers in traditional versions. Over the whole is cast the air of tragic irony;

human complaint is too puny to trouble the makers of destiny. Mark's words, on hearing from Iseult that Tristram is dead, are a cry from the depths of man's impotence:

> *He has died too many many times*
> *For that report to hold! In tilts, in frays,*
> *Through slits and loops, louvres and battlements,*
> *Has he been pierced and arrowed to the heart,*
> *Then risen up again to trouble me!*[12]

Yet as in Hardy's novels and much of his poetry, a sense of strong if astringent compassion works in the play. In keeping with the classical mode, tragic emotion is distilled through the words of those outside the action. In the Prologue, Merlin, a witness to all the events, "being ageless, deathless," urges that the lovers be not judged harshly:

> *Sorrow therein they tasted of,*
> *And deeply, and too long!*

A "Chorus of Shades of Dead Cornish Men and Women" also helps to purify the anguish of the lovers by the pity and understanding of those who stand beyond life. Hardy's play, therefore, has something of the lofty and almost abstract quality of classical tragedy, working within situations unpretentious in characterization and dramatic structure.

Like Hardy's *Famous Tragedy*, John Masefield's play *Tristan and Isolt* (1927) follows some of the older ways. His play reveals a deep and respectful interest in the ancient British form of the story, and combines what might be called fossilized fragments of the tale with the great medieval episodes. Apart from the erratic effect of some of the experiments, *Tristan and Isolt* makes good reading.

Masefield's devotion to the Arthurian story is of long standing. As a young man, while working in a carpet factory in Yonkers, New York, he first read Malory, "straight through, with growing pleasure." The story, and Caxton's Preface, moved him deeply. He had no doubt that Arthur had once lived, and he hoped that some manuscript might be discovered to prove it.[13] This attitude of trust and hopefulness has happily never quite left him. It appears in his desire, strongly marked even in recent years, to learn what he can about the primitive forms of the legend, those tales which may have been attached to a real Arthur or Tristram.[14]

The story of the Cornish lovers especially caught his imagination. His *Tristan and Isolt* had its immediate origin in Joseph Bédier's critical study of the early legend, and in the researches of J. Loth. To a studious interest in the history and early forms of the story was added the influence of association with legendary sites in Cornwall. During visits to the land of Lyonesse, especially near Truro and Redruth, he was stirred by surviving landmarks of the legend: the barrow reputed to be the tomb of Mark, the stone supposed to mark Tristram's grave, and the river crossing named after "Essyllt."[15] These reminders of a heroic age worked strongly in the mind of the man who had read the *Morte Darthur* in his youth with something like Keats's ramping delight in *The Faerie Queene*.

Masefield's play, which begins with an account of Tristan's parentage and ends with the death of the lovers, is fresh and unhackneyed in treatment. It returns to the ancient Pictish and Welsh springs of the legend. Tristan is the son of King Tallorc and the Princess Olwen, daughter of King Meirchyon of Cornwall, whose lands the pirate Kolbein had seized, and whose son Marc he had reduced to ignominious vassalage.[16] Kolbein, who murders not only Meirchyon but Tallorc as well, serves an appropriate function in the story by fighting a mortal

duel with Tristan, in place of the usual Morolt. Thus the somewhat casual trial by combat of the traditional versions becomes
an act of vengeance in which Tristan exacts retribution for the
destruction Kolbein has inflicted on his family. The tragic train
of consequences is further knit together by Kolbein's dying
request that his daughter Isolt be brought by Tristan from
Ireland, where she lives with her mother, Queen Thurid, to
be married to the man he has wronged, Marc of Cornwall.
Thereafter the story follows the general outline laid down by
previous narrators — with a few differences. Like Béroul and
Malory, Masefield ties the stories of Arthur and Tristan together, though in this case Arthur is not a king but rather the
dux bellorum of the ancient story, the captain of a Romano-
British army, who comes to Kolbein to seek his aid in war
against the heathen. A further primitive touch is found in the
fact that Kai and Bedwyr act as spies and informers upon the
lovers. Masefield here remembers that curious scene in the
Welsh *Triads* in which Kay and Bedivere, with Marc and
Arthur, try to steal swine from the herd Tristan is guarding
in place of the regular swineherd, who has gone on an urgent
errand to Essyllt. Indeed this scene is thrust bodily into the
present play, and Kai and Bedwyr continue to plot throughout *Tristan and Isolt*.[17] Details of this kind, and such little-
used episodes from the early stories as the meal spread on the
floor of Isolt's room to reveal Tristan's footprints, and the
"water of ordeal" which Marc demands that Isolt drink, are
clear proof of Masefield's interest in the ancient forms of the
story.

The play, however, is more than a series of experiments.
Tristan and Isolt widens the world of the lovers beyond the
ecstasy and tragedy of love. These last elements are strongly
present of course, as they must be. Yet the lovers are not

simply prisoners of their passion; they also are part of a larger kingdom whose people see other issues than consuming emotion. In this sense Masefield is more traditional in his treatment than most contemporary retellers of the legend. Though he does not approach the shambling prolixity, the profuse and often ill-assorted detail of the Tristram story in Malory, he sets the tale in a large framework which shall include but not be absorbed by passionate love. National issues are kept before the reader's eyes. Arthur, the Romano-British captain, who first comes to Cornwall to seek Kolbein's help against the heathen, eventually wins the support of Marc, who, by a daring change in the story, dies in the great victory at Badon Hill. Thus Marc has national responsibilities on his mind as well as his wife's unfaithfulness. Arthur also has more important things to do than join Kai and Bedwyr in trapping a pair of adulterers. Furthermore, Tristan has obligations other than love. As the son of Tallorc he is a king in his own right, and his friend Dinan makes it clear that his duty lies with his own people and not with Isolt. The national issue comes into head-on collision with the personal, for Dinan urges Tristan to assume leadership of his people, who are also threatened by the heathen; furthermore he tells him that his subjects will have none of Isolt. They demand an unspotted Queen. The upshot of these arguments is the expected one: Tristan remains steadfast to Isolt. Throughout the play the obligations of the outer world add their weight to internal stresses and strains. In addition, Masefield's suggestions that there are other people in Cornwall besides lords and ladies relax the tensions of the story and temper the violence of love-madness. Much is made of Tristan's adventure as the temporary guardian of Hog the swineherd's pigs. Perhaps the episode is out of key with the rest of the story; certainly it seems too long.[18]

Again it reveals, however, Masefield's intention to let the story expand to what he considers a natural point of repose, not only by recognizing the sort of rough foolery which must have been a part of a primitive society but also by a tacit assumption that simple folk touched the fringes of the ancient knightly world. As a final point it is worth noting that Tristan is attended in his mortal illness not by Isolt of the White Hands (who plays no part in the story) but by the rustic maiden Pixne.

Although the lovers move in a world somewhat larger than usual, yet their mutual passion is the focus of their lives. Masefield's eclecticism, his refusal to hold closely to the formula of whatever age at the expense of elasticity and fresh invention, is revealed in his approach to Tristan and Isolt themselves. In keeping with modern practice, they are more vivid as individuals than their counterparts of medieval romance. As a necessary result one does not often hear the high romantic note of chivalric love. The speech of the lovers makes little use of lofty declamation. Even so, Masefield avoids the centripetal, introverted tension which marks so much analysis of character in our day. Tristan and Isolt are passionate, violent, and somewhat unpredictable. At times they hurt one another cruelly. But the reader need not seek for explanations in terms of "neurotic ambivalence" or morbid fixations or any of the other apparatus of abnormal psychology. They act not like the patients of a psychiatrist but rather like the mercurial persons they undoubtedly were. They are almost completely free of agonized self-analysis and self-pity. Consequently they strike the reader as individuals who, though hopelessly enmeshed in tragedy, still have human elasticity, even at times to the point of the cruelty which seizes upon wild beasts newly caged. Few scenes in the Tristram legend can surpass Masefield's account of the agonized moments when Tristan learns from Isolt that she must lie in Marc's marriage bed. And even the familiar substitution of Brangwen in the Queen's place only temporarily relieves a pressure that continues to the very end. Forceful also is the episode describing Isolt's return to Marc, after the King has discovered the sleeping lovers in the forest cave and has magnanimously spared them. Isolt's pangs of conscience at the forbearance of her husband send her back to him in a turmoil of repentance. In almost hysterical determination she says that she has "bolted the bars on love." Tristan, shaken to the core by Isolt's defection, for a time goes mad. Only at the end, after Marc has fallen at Badon Hill and Tristan lies ill and dying in the forest,[19] are the lovers truly united, and then only for their last farewell. Here their passions resolve and purify themselves, and death comes in high nobility, as if the waves of the stormy ocean which beat on Tintagel were now a murmur on the moonlit shingle. All passion spent, Isolt resolves on her suicide:

> *I am following, Tristan;*
> *Wait for your cruel killer, a little hour.*
> *You shall be my death as I have been yours, beloved.*
> *We who have flooded like the Severn, will ebb*
> *To the great sea together like tides going out.*[20]

At Arthur's command the lovers are buried where they had died; his simple words send them into the light:

> *We will bury them together, here where they lie.*
> *If they have sinned, they have loved with a love exceeding:*
> *Now they are spirits of love, not bodies bleeding.*[21]

So ends Masefield's tragedy of the Cornish lovers. Revealing the elasticity of the author's narrative invention, and his interest in the ancient sources of the legend, it describes lovers of flesh and blood, doomed by their passion yet creatures of will in a world greater than themselves.[22]

When we pass from Kendon and Hardy and Masefield to other modern versions of the Tristram legend we enter a new world. As early as 1917 Arthur Symons had prepared us for neurotic involution, yet for a time his voice was not clearly heard by the reworkers of the Tristram story. In the group which remains, however, all of whom abandon the dramatic form often used in the twentieth century, the intense, brittle world of our own experience is very much with us.

In one of these works the modern tone is found not so much in the peculiarly taut, psychological *Weltschmerz* of the twentieth century as in mocking raillery and cynical sophistication. Even as early as 1926, John Erskine had tried in *Galahad* to make the land of Logres seem as smart and up-to-date as a Park Avenue drawing room. In *Tristan and Isolde* (1932) he transfers the world of fashionable intrigue to Lyonesse.

The subtitle of the novel is "Restoring Palamede," and it is really Palamede's story as much as Tristan's or Isolde's. As T. H. White was to do later and with more originality and wit in *The Witch in the Wood*, Erskine has transformed Malory's sketch of the confused paynim Palomides into a full-length portrait.

Palamede, a nobly born young Arab, has heard such glowing tales of knighthood and the beautiful women in Brittany from a Christian slave that he sails for the West. On reaching France, however, his ardor is considerably cooled by ugly women and unchivalrous men, and he turns to Cornwall. There he finds himself caught up in the affairs of Tristan and Isolde, at about the time of Isolde's marriage to Mark. As in Malory, Palamede falls hopelessly in love with the Irish Princess, and, by way of additional embarrassment, Brangain, Isolde's handsome cousin, with him. The story then pursues a somewhat complicated course, introducing many traditional situations and new glimpses of fashionable intrigue and adultery. Palamede rather than Mark occupies the apex of the triangle. It is he who mortally wounds Tristan after he has fled Cornwall and married Isolde of Brittany. His pangs of adjustment in a confusing, alien society bulk larger in the novel than the throes of the lovers.

Erskine's changes wrench the story badly. Again, as in *Galahad*, he cannot seem to decide whether he wishes to be grave or gay. Lacking Bernard Shaw's gift for being magnificently foolish and wise at one and the same time he achieves only a kind of neon flashiness. The end of the story finds Tristan dead by his rival's sword and Isolde desolate. Yet even here Erskine cannot avoid the slick and easy dramatic turn. Palamede departs, to take ship for the East. Brangain, hearing of it, cries out "Where is the Holy Land? Get me a horse!" And so this modern "Tragedy of Cornwall" ends neither with a bang nor a whimper, but a wisecrack!

The shift in emphasis to Palamede has disastrous effects, particularly on the men. Isolde and Brangain fare pretty well. Isolde, passionate, occasionally cruel and unpredictable, is a real person; Brangain is quite believable as the steadfast yet spirited handmaiden. Palamede's crescent ascendant, however, means a great dimming of Tristan's star. The paynim burns with the flame of passion more than the knight of Cornwall. Tristan, therefore, is reduced, if not in Isolde's eyes then in the eyes of the reader and of many who knew him, to a kind of adolescent capriciousness. He is a brash and cocky young man, content to go his own erratic way whenever he wishes, finding sport in the easy charms of Phenice and Belinde. Possibly Erskine chose to exaggerate Malory's picture of Tristram in his early days as a rather carefree young buck not above an affair with the wife of Sir Segwarides, but if so, he followed a bad lead. Generations of the faithful reject Tristram as a casual amorist. King Mark is also transmogrified. He is of course ridiculed — that goes without saying; but it is too much to find this absurd cuckold storming like the choleric colonel in *Punch*.

These changes, though dictated by an age which has half believed Bernard Shaw as to the stupidity of the male and the dominance of the female, play hob with the old strength of the legend. The passion which moved Tristan and Isolde to their doom becomes dissipated in a welter of castle gossip and interminable talky-talk. The characters purport to be figures in a heroic legend, but they can never forget that they are also modern sophisticates, strolling in costume amid Erskine's alien corn.

The Tristram story serves the needs of contemporary experience also in two other novels: Charles Morgan's *Sparkenbroke* (1936) and Mary Ellen Chase's *Dawn in Lyonesse* (1938). In each the tragedy of the Cornish lovers is a symbolic background for a modern tale. *Sparkenbroke* is a long, reflective, and analytical account of Piers Tenniel, Viscount Sparkenbroke, and his love for Mary Leward. His relations with Mary (later married to Dr. George Hardy) are vaguely colored by the fact that he is writing a novel about Tristan and Isolt. Yet the implied parallels between Sparkenbroke, Mary, and Hardy, and the Cornish trio are not clear; for all its shadowy suggestions of heroic adventure the tale seems the usual one of triangular love. And Sparkenbroke as Tristan is more of a Byronic hero than anywhere else in the legend, with the possible exception of Malory.

Miss Chase's novel is equally vague and tentative. The heroine, Ellen Pascoe, a woman in her thirties, is a waitress at the "King Arthur's Castle Hotel," Tintagel. Deeply stirred by reading of Tristram and Isolt in a book provided for the guests, she apparently thinks of her attachment to the fisherman, Derek Tregonny, in terms of the old legend. When Derek is lost at sea and when Ellen's friend Susan Pengilly confesses her misconduct with him the story dissolves in a blur of high-minded forgiveness. As in *Sparkenbroke,* the parallel to the Cornish story is not close. Miss Chase attempts to give the feel of the old days by "atmospheric" scenes, emphasizing the rugged, romantic landscape near Tintagel, and the shadowy traditions which haunt the place. Such passages, however, seem self-conscious and overwritten, and add little to what is rather a pale story.

In Hannah Closs's novel *Tristan* (1940) the legend returns to ancient Cornwall. The land and its people, however, are seen through modern eyes, not the rather mocking eyes of John Erskine, but those of an author who cannot escape from the nervous involution of modern living.

Though Mrs. Closs's story covers a wide range, following Tristan from his boyhood and through most of the traditional episodes down to his death, it strikes one not so much with its width as with a self-conscious and almost querulous introversion. This tone is one of several ways in which *Tristan* reflects our age. The supernatural element, for example, is completely eliminated. True, Tristan reflects on the story of Parzival and the Grail, yet one gathers that he is thinking of a legend in the mythological past.[23] Early in life the supernatural turns into reality for him when the "dragon" he has slain turns out to be a seal. Most important of all, the love potion disappears. Furthermore, the political aspects of the story are emphasized far more than usual. There is much talk, for example, of how well or ill Tristan's father, Rivalin, ruled Lyonesse. And Tristan himself, after Iseult's marriage to Marc, returns to his homeland and sets it in order. At another crucial point in his career he resolves a crisis by pacifying the rebellious land of Brittany and re-establishing the young Kaherdin in power. Mrs. Closs even gives us a few brief glimpses of the common people, particularly in one scene describing the brutal treatment of an old farmer who has not paid his tithe.

Yet these attempts to enlarge the world beyond the circle of passion, as Masefield had done in *Tristan and Isolt,* are not of great consequence in Mrs. Closs's novel because the lovers themselves are narrowly confined. The measure of greatness in the "Tragedy of Cornwall" must always rest on the success with which suffering is transformed into soaring and purifying passion. In Mrs. Closs's story the sense of purification and tragic justification is lacking, for she tends to overstress the psychological and intuitional aspects of character. A suggestion of this attitude is found in the Introduction, in which she justifies her choice of the novel rather than drama in treating the story:

Is not much of the poignancy of the tragedy lost in modern versions because so often they adopt the dramatic form, thus hardly allowing us to remember that Tristan was once a boy, a child, and that in his childhood is already foreshadowed his fatality?[24]

Probing into behavior marks the author's method throughout. Indeed one feels that Guenelon's words about Tristan make probing a necessity: "There was always a secret life in him, [which] kept him a stranger from his fellows."[25] In thus using interior reflection to reveal the "secret life" of her protagonists Mrs. Closs changes the emphasis and contracts the scope of the tragedy. It is not that Tristan and Iseult are unreal. At times, through flashes of insight they are even vivid. Yet the tragedy is less a march than a tableau; the story has a static and meditative quality which matches ill with the high events of passionate doom. Said a reviewer in the *Times Literary Supplement,* "The intricate delvings into the mind of each of the lovers destroy the unity of their meaning for each other, and the massive sweep is disintegrated."[26] The "massive sweep" is indeed lacking in Mrs. Closs's novel. Tristan and Iseult seem caged within themselves, their private pangs exposed in a self-conscious, allusive manner of writing which often obscures the sequence of events and reduces the catastrophic and cathartic strength of the tragedy.[27]

The most recent American novel to deal with Tristram is *The Enchanted Cup* (1953) by Dorothy James Roberts, who became interested in the legend while doing graduate work at the University of Wisconsin under a student of Joseph Bédier. Nevertheless she bases her story largely on Malory rather than the medieval writers Bédier used in making his excellent reconstruction. *The Enchanted Cup* follows Tristram from infancy to his death at the hands of Mark. In a way it is a return to older forms, for it stresses the varied, adventurous career of the hero. Like other contemporary writers, Miss Roberts tries to make her story credible to modern readers. Her language is mercifully free of bastard medieval and she is at pains to use simple, rude details of "real" life. As might be expected, the supernatural plays no part. In fact the title of the novel is misleading, for the love potion seems to be explained as Irish superstition. Tristram takes no stock in its magical power. Thus it serves no real function in the story, especially since the lovers are already deeply committed. The love story is the least effective part of the novel. Both Tristram and Isoud are conventional types: Tristram never happier than when he has a sword in his hand, Isoud the slim princess of what might have been in earlier novels a mythical Balkan kingdom. As a tale of adventure, however, *The Enchanted Cup* moves along smoothly, and Miss Roberts has the narrative sense to make some of the sharp turns in the story convincing.

From the novelists to E. A. Robinson is a wide leap! True, most of them, like him, are modern in their concentration on the inner life of their characters. It is this approach, indeed, which probably makes Robinson's *Tristram* less moving than *Merlin* or *Lancelot;* the torments of the lovers often seem private woe rather than mounting tragedy. Yet its brilliant psychological insight, its compassion, its clean strength of expression, and its tightness of structure give the poem a high place.[28]

Long before the publication of *Tristram* in 1927 the story had fascinated Robinson. In his early New York days his imagination was deeply stirred by Wagner's *Tristan und Isolde,* so much so that he gave as a reason for not escaping to Madagascar the fact that he would have to do without *Tristan.* His wardrobe even suffered through his devotion, when, instead of buying a new pair of trousers, he spent the money for a performance of the opera at the Metropolitan.[29] Later, during serene and fruitful years at Peterborough, he asked his friend Isaacs to bring him some music, mentioning especially *Tristan* and others by Wagner.[30] It was during this period of his career that the legend pressed on him to be written. In a letter written from Peterborough in June, 1925, to his friend Craven Langstroth Betts, Robinson says:

I came down here with every intention of writing some short things for a new book, but our old friend Tristram, whom I have been fighting off for some five years, got me finally by the throat and refused to let go.[31]

On its publication in 1927 *Tristram* was an immediate success. The critics were virtually unanimous in praise, and the poem rapidly became a best seller. Selected by the Literary Guild as the "book-of-the-month" it was reprinted four times in three weeks, twelve times within the year. A crowd of notables gathered in a public reception at the Little Theatre in New York to honor Robinson; in due course *Tristram* received the accolade of the Pulitzer Prize. With the possible exception of Tennyson's *Idylls,* never before had an Arthurian story aroused such widespread enthusiasm.

The story begins in Brittany, where Isolt of the White Hands patiently waits for the return of Tristram, who had visited her country some time before. Then to Cornwall — and Isolt of Ireland's wedding night. In spite of the urging of Gouvernail and Queen Morgan, Tristram angrily and despairingly refuses to attend the nuptial feast. Isolt and Brangwaine then come to him, and there follows an ardent love scene, observed by Andred, who is roughly handled when discovered by Tristram. At this point King Mark enters and angrily banishes Tristram from the kingdom. For a time he lives, dazed, in the woods. After a brief interlude when Queen Morgan tries unsuccessfully to make him forget Isolt, he leaves for Brittany, where he helps King Howel in stabilizing his land. There he marries Howel's daughter, the whitehanded Isolt. Eventually, in spite of his wife's fears, he goes to Arthur's court with Gawaine, to be made a knight of the Round Table. A meeting is arranged between Tristram and Isolt at Lancelot's castle, Joyous Gard (Mark being then in prison), and there follow idyllic summer months together. But their joy comes to a rude end: Mark, released from prison, captures Isolt. Terrible days ensue for Tristram, so terrible that even Mark is moved by pity to allow the lovers to see each other again. There follows a bittersweet reunion, darkened always by the shadow of the realization that eventually Tristram will return to his wife in Brittany. But even this is denied; Tristram and Isolt fall under Andred's dagger; King Mark, stunned and shocked beyond measure, sends word to Howel. The poem ends with Isolt of the White Hands gazing out over an empty sea.

As will be evident from the summary, Robinson has used traditional material from a number of predecessors in fashioning his story of the doomed lovers. Yet when we say that in general he follows Malory — the association of Tristram with Arthur's knights, the introduction of the uncommon episodes concerning Morgan le Fay, the denigration of Mark (though he improves at the end, and, contrary to Malory, does not kill Tristram) — that he suggests Wagner in the murder of Tristram by one of Mark's spies; that, like Arnold, he gives Isolt of Ireland black hair; we are stating only surface facts about the poem. Its importance in the history of the legend lies in its completely individual synthesis of old material.

There are a number of reasons why Robinson's *Tristram* so stirred the American reading public of the late twenties. Its extraordinary concentration appealed strongly to a generation which had looked at life more often through the microscope than the telescope. Also, as in all of Robinson's poems, there is a kind of innate honesty and lack of pretense in *Tristram;* one sees the story "as it actually was," or rather as it actually would be if the lovers were living today. Furthermore, though it is true poetry, it is a singularly "unpoetized" version of the legend. The older conventions — passages of set description or daring combat or declamatory apostrophes — are almost completely lacking. Gone is the sensuous extravagance of Swinburne, the metaphysical passion of Wagner. Gone also are the crowded incidents of the early versions.[32]

Robinson not only compresses the story into the space between the marriage of Isolt to Mark and the death of the lovers but he also subordinates the incidents strictly to the internal conflicts of Tristram and Isolt themselves. In keeping with the temper of his age and his own skepticism Robinson eliminates the love potion completely. A letter to his friend Mrs. Richards reveals his reason:

The fool potion or philtre in the Tristram story has always been an incurable source of annoyance to me. [He meant to tell, he continues] what might have happened to human beings in those circumstances, without their wits and wills having been taken away by some impossible and wholly superfluous concoction. Men and women can make trouble enough for themselves without being denatured and turned into rabbits.[33]

Though the statement that the love potion dehumanizes the lovers can be argued, certainly Robinson's Tristram and Isolt are neither "denatured" nor "turned into rabbits." They are entirely lifelike people. Yet one may wonder whether their reality has not been won at too heavy a cost. Robinson's refusal to use the love potion has altered not only the motivation of the story but also a means by which love is raised to superhuman heights. Flights of mounting passion, of complete union in love, are rarer in *Tristram* than in most of the other great versions; instead we see the lovers harried and agonized by a love which beats against the bars of its self-made prison. Only once do we really see them completely and happily at one, in the idyllic summer weeks at Joyous Gard. Here the waves of love, of the sort springing from the potion in others of the tales, overwhelm them in a great tide. For the rest, they are tossed in agony, the prey of their all too human desire, their all too human conscience at the ghastly dilemma for which they are responsible. No gods are wreaking their vengeance on them; Tristram and Isolt act alone in their world. Only Fate moves darkly above and beyond — Fate

> *which must itself*
> *Be but a monstrous and unholy jest.*[34]

In no other version of the legend has the suffering of the lovers been so movingly and even harrowingly portrayed. Tristram is a haunted man in the world of his own insecurities. Isolt sees him perhaps more clearly than he sees himself:

> *Something in you was always in my father:*
> *A darkness always was around my father,*
> *...He saw*
> *Nothing, but he would see the shadow of it*
> *Before he saw the color or shape it had,*
> *Or where the sun was.*[35]

His imagination, stirred to its depths by the love he can never fully achieve, turns inward in masochistic frenzy. Never before had Tristram's agony on Isolt's wedding night been described with such intensity:

> *Before long now*
> *That music and that wordless murmuring*
> *Of distant men and women, who divined*
> *As much or little as they might, would cease;*
> *The mocking lights above him would go out;*
> *There would be silence; and the King would hold*
> *Isolt — Isolt of the dark eyes — Isolt*
> *Of the patrician passionate helplessness —*
> *Isolt of the soft waving blue-black hair —*

Isolt of Ireland — in his vicious arms
And crush the bloom of her resisting life
On his hot, watery mouth, and overcome
The protest of her suffering silk skin
With his crude senile claws. And it was he,
Tristram, the loud-accredited strong warrior,
Tristram, the loved of women, the harp-player,
Tristram, the learned Nimrod among hunters,
Tristram, the most obedient imbecile
And humble servant of King Mark his uncle,
Who had achieved all this. For lack of sight
And sense of self, and imperturbably,
He had achieved all this and might do more,
No doubt, if given the time. Whereat he cursed
Himself again, and his complacent years
Of easy blindness. Time had saved for him
The flower that he had not the wit to seize
And carry a few leagues across the water,
Till when he did so it was his no more,
And body and soul were sick to think of it.
Why should he not be sick? "Good God in heaven,"
He groaned aloud, "why should I not be sick!"[36]

At times, one suspects, Tristram needs his own suffering almost as much as he needs Isolt; he is a man who must live at war with himself. Isolt, on the other hand, is the more objective and the more successfully loving of the two. She is indeed the most admirable of all Robinson's Arthurian women, an exception to his troublemaking, provocative females.[37] Though no less devoted than Tristram she seems more clear-eyed, more elastic than he. Tristram moves almost like one in a dream. Though we are led to believe that he is a man of action, he is so bound to his inner agony that his will to act has been cruelly restricted. With him, love for Isolt is all or nothing; Isolt, on the other hand, sees farther than the ecstatic moment, even to the dark necessity of enduring without love. It is she who prophesies the end of their idyllic days at Joyous Gard:

> *There is your world outside, all fame and banners,*
> *And it was never mine to take from you.*
> *You must not let me take your world away*
> *From you, after all this. Love is not that.*
> *Before you are much older, I suppose*
> *You will go back to Brittany, where Isolt —*
> *That other Isolt — will think, and some day know.*
> *Women are not so bitter if once they know,*
> *And if the other is dead. Now forget that,*
> *And kiss me as if we were to live forever.*
> *Perhaps we shall, somewhere.*[38]

Isolt is a woman of insight and judgment, eager to give her lover all the freedom he needs to take his rightful place in the world, because she knows that their love is a bond between them. Even in the moment of their final parting, she drains the bitter cup of resignation; it is she who stands above their passion and sees them both as they are:

> *Lying with eyes closed*
> *And all her senses tired with pain and love,*
> *And pity for love that was to die, she saw him*
> *More as a thunder-stricken tower of life*
> *Brought down by fire, than as a stricken man*
> *Brought down by fate, and always to wear scars*
> *That in his eyes and voice were changelessly*
> *Revealed and hidden. There was another voice,*
> *Telling of when there should be left for him*
> *No place among the living any longer;*
> *And there was peace and wisdom, saying to her,*

It will be best then, when it is all done.
But her own peace and wisdom frightened her,
And she would see him only as he had been
Before. That was the best for her to see;
And it was best that each should see the other
Unseen, and as they were before the world
Was done with them, and for a little while,
In silence, to forget and to remember.[39]

A moment later, under the knife of Andred, the world is done with them both. Yet in the silence which envelops them there quivers the faint music of peace and remembrance. The endurance of Isolt has purified and ennobled the suffering of Tristram.

It is the women who see the farthest in Robinson's *Tristram*. To Tristram himself love was too immediate and too terrible a problem; to Mark, the "man-shaped goat," a king whose coarseness is but little redeemed by his stunned comprehension at the final tragedy, true love, indeed any kind of passion save the physical, was meaningless; even the faithful Gouvernail is bewildered by his master's agonies. His remark on seeing Tristram well-nigh out of his mind when Mark abducts Isolt from Joyous Gard says much in little:

> *If this be love,*
> *May I grow merry and old and amiable*
> *On hate.*[40]

For Robinson's men, especially for a poet who had never known the rewards of high passion, love was not only an insoluble mystery but also a continuous and not often delicious torment. As Emery Neff says, "requited passion lay outside [Robinson's] experience."[41] This makes all the more remarkable Robinson's respect for the selfless devotion of women.

79

Feminine devotion is enhanced dramatically by the conflicting claims of the two Isolts. Here we have two kinds of love, each admirable and necessary in its own way, playing against one another. The balance is by no means overwhelmingly in Isolt of Ireland's favor, for Isolt of Brittany stands high in Robinson's regard. If her reticent inwardness was a perplexity to her father, King Howel, who compared her to "a changeling down from one of those white stars," if her gentle devotion was an embarrassment to Tristram, certainly she is far from the supine figure some authors have made her. Isolt of Brittany has a dignity which gives her a poignant appeal. Like her rival she loves with her eyes open: she knows what she may expect and what she may not:

> *"If I lost you*
> *For a long time," she said, with her insistence,*
> *"I should not cry for what had come between,*
> *For I should have you here with me again.*
> *I am not one who must have everything.*
> *I was not fated to have everything.*
> *One may be wise enough, not having all,*
> *Still to be found among the fortunate."*[42]

Perhaps even more than her namesake of Ireland, it is she who embodies the stoicism which marks Robinson's attitude toward the drama of life.[43] In a sense she frames the tragedy: the story opens with her awaiting the return of Tristram to Brittany after his first visit; it ends with her gazing at the sea over which Tristram would never come to her again. White birds are flying, the sunlight flashes on the waters, and the turbulence of love is touched by an autumnal calm. It is no peace of exhaustion that holds Isolt of Brittany; probably it is not peace at all, but rather that endurance through hardships which Robinson (like Joseph Conrad) believed to be the highest victory of man. Isolt of Ireland died for her love; Isolt of Brittany had to live without it.

So ends Robinson's "Tragedy of Cornwall," in the judgment of some critics the best version of the legend in the English language. It deserves a high place because of the extraordinarily vivid and compassionate picture of the lovers caught up in a frenzy which destroys them, and also because of Robinson's insistence upon purity of form and idea. In *Tristram* the passion is distilled, for the emotion, powerful as it is, is always subject to a stoic discipline. The very style itself is distilled. Though Robinson is by no means incapable of lyrical feeling, for the most part the language is remarkably taut and unsensuous.

Yet with all its virtues *Tristram* is not the most successful of Robinson's Arthurian poems. The reasons probably lie in the modern change of emphasis on Tristram's place in the story and in Robinson's stress on the conflicts of love rather than its rewards.

In the medieval romances and in Malory, Tristram is not only a great lover, but a superlative harper, a highly skilled hunter, and a mighty knight in combat. He is a man of outstanding ability in fields which commanded the attention of vigorous men in medieval society. He was a man of action before he became a lover, and he continued so even after he met Isolt. The early versions of the story, therefore, are a little less obsessively concentrated on one side of his career than more recent ones. Even since Victorian times, however, Tristram has been more lover than chivalric hero (though of course the two are not mutually exclusive). Tennyson's degradation of him in "The Last Tournament" did rank injustice to a man of great parts; Arnold showed little of his chivalric élan and versatility, and Swinburne emphasized sensuous and

emotional aspects of the story more than ever before. With a
few exceptions, authors of our time have intensified the restric-
tion of Tristram within the limits of Courtly Love, as modernly
conceived, suggesting his other capabilities by reminiscence
and allusion. All this means a definite change, and some loss,
in the story itself. The stately and rather naive idealism of the
Middle Ages has been much altered; the pageant of chivalric
action has largely gone. Instead the attention is centered on
the love itself, as it reveals complex psychological responses
in the minds of the protagonists. This is especially true of
Robinson. He concentrates very skillfully on the emotions of
the lovers, but too often at the cost of loquacious analysis.[44]
Action and incident which heretofore have added excitement
to the story are reduced to a minimum; the tension is almost
wholly psychological.

As an astringent commentary on love *Tristram* is without
equal in the history of the legend. Save in one section it is
very different from Wagner's *Tristan und Isolde,* which Robinson much admired. Francis Fergusson says of *Tristan und
Isolde* that it is "not so much a love-story as it is the celebration of a mystical motive; not the story of a passion, as we
observe it realistically, . . . but the mystic obedience to passion
itself."[45] Robinson found this mystical obedience hard to give.
Only in the description of Tristram and Isolt's blissful days at
Joyous Gard do we find release in passion which knows no
time, place, or end. After that the lovers seem to surrender to
hard Fate. In the "Liebestod," *Tristan und Isolde* ends with
the overwhelming triumph of devotion over death; *Tristram*
comes to a close with stoic resignation, with peace for the
lovers rather than fulfillment – a solace as austere as Lancelot's
bleak comfort in the "Light" of the Grail. Once Robinson had
released his feeling in the description of the days at Joyous

Gard it is as though he repented of his surrender, and took refuge once again in the virtue of endurance under suffering. Remembering his deep skepticism we can guess that much as he was moved by *Tristan und Isolde* he distrusted its glorification of mystical devotion. In *Tristram*, therefore, peace seems to have come without victory. Like his own Merlin, Robinson at the last turned his back on love as an end in itself.

No catalogue of exceptions, however, can lessen the importance of Robinson's *Tristram*, for it is a magnificent addition to the legend. In a letter written to Harry De Forest Smith, May 13, 1896, Robinson says: "I am inclined to be a trifle solemn in my verses, but I intend that there shall always be at least a suggestion of something wiser than hatred and something better than despair."[46] This doctrine, pursued throughout the poet's whole career, throws *Tristram* into high relief. It is a work nobly conceived and executed, dominated always by that classic *gravitas* which underlies any tragic art worthy of the name, transforming Mark's hatred into understanding, and the despair of the lovers into a source of strength to other men and women. Endurance which brings wisdom and peace with it — this is the tough ethical fiber of the poem. Isolt of Brittany is Robinson's spokesman in her words to her father near the close of the poem:

> *Wisdom is not one word and then another,*
> *Till words are like dry leaves under a tree;*
> *Wisdom is like a dawn that comes up slowly*
> *Out of an unknown ocean.*[47]

Dux Bellorum

Tunc Arthur pugnabat contr' illos in illis diebus
cum regibus Brittonum, sed ipse dux erat bellorum.[1]
— NENNIUS, *Historia Britonum*

The twentieth century has not always been content to leave Arthur enthroned as a medieval monarch, in the great tradition of Geoffrey, Malory, and Tennyson. Contemporary novelists have added fresh and original material to the legend in "modernizing" Arthur by making him more ancient; in other words, by reviving the shadowy Celt who probably fought against the Germanic invaders of Britain in the sixth century. As he appears in Nennius' chronicle — to be sure somewhat after the fact, since it was probably written in the ninth century — he is not a king but a military commander who defeated the Anglo-Saxons in a series of twelve battles. The passage in Nennius and other references in early Celtic literature make it probable that there was a historic Arthur, though indeed he is still but the shadow of a name. Possibly Nennius created his *dux bellorum* from legends which may have gathered about Artorius Castus, an eminent Roman

soldier of the second century A.D., whose sarcophagus, discovered at Spalato, on the Adriatic, was inscribed with an
account of his life, including his service in Britain with the
famous Sixth Legion. However that may be, whether Arthur
was a Roman or a Romanized Briton or a Celt through and
through, he was a soldier so successful that his name became
the focus for more and more elaborate legend.

The creation of a new, "historic" Arthur was an experiment
which writers of our time could hardly be expected to resist.
Historical fiction had flourished in the nineteenth century, and
continued to do so in the twentieth. When a primitive Arthur
was revealed by scholarly research a whole new world lay
before the re-creators of the legend. They now had the oppor-
tunity of adding the freshness of "historical realism" to a figure
who had lived in Celtic Britain as well as in Camelot.

The full-blown *dux bellorum* of our day emerges rather
slowly from erratic, romanticized pictures of him and his time
in earlier historical novels, often written for children. Easily
the best of this early group is Bishop and Brodeur's *The Altar
of the Legion* — a good yarn. Before the publication of W.
Barnard Faraday's *Pendragon* in 1930 there is practically no
attempt to deal with the subject realistically. After this, however, Arthur and sixth-century Britain stand out clearly.

Of the forerunners the earliest seems to have been the
Reverend Alfred J. Church, an English classical scholar and
author of romances for children, who set one of his stories in
Roman Britain.[2] *The Count of the Saxon Shore, or, the Villa
in Vectis: A Tale of the Departure of the Romans from Britain*
(1887), as its formidable title indicates, deals mostly with the
dark period which immediately preceded the great victories
of Arthur. Though it may have appealed to children of Vic-
toria's time, modern readers of whatever age will find it a

85

hard chore. Church tries to give some of the historical flavor of the age but succeeds only in sticking occasional raisins of antiquarian detail into a soggy rice pudding. Of *Celtic* Britain or its people we see practically nothing. Most of the story concerns the Romanized Briton, Aelius, Count of the Saxon Shore, who moves through a series of sentimental, melodramatic incidents. Arthur appears briefly at the close of the story, to arrange a marriage between Carna, the daughter of Aelius, and the mortally wounded Saxon slave, Cedric. This bittersweet event immediately follows Arthur's great victory over the Saxons at Badon Hill. Yet even though Church tells us practically nothing about either the man or his greatest battle, he does make Arthur a war-leader (not a King) in Roman Britain of the fifth century, and this in the very days of Tennyson.[3]

Warwick Deeping apparently found Roman Britain an alluring field for fanciful romances. Three of his novels, *Uther and Igraine* (1902), *The Man on the White Horse* (1934), and *The Man Who Went Back* (1940), take us to the Britain of Arthur's day.[4]

Uther and Igraine, as the title indicates, is a story of Arthur's parents. In common with so many others, Deeping goes to Malory for fresh material, but there are those who would prefer the tale in the *Morte Darthur,* crude and primitive though it is, to a color-added romance of Roman Britain. The story begins well before the marriage of the two, when Uther rescues Igraine from Saxon invaders. As in Malory, Gorlois of Cornwall is Uther's rival. In a startling change from the original, Merlin's magic brings about Igraine's marriage not to Uther but to Gorlois. This embarrassment is overcome, however, during the siege of Tintagel, when Uther kills his rival in single combat. Deeping makes some effort to give legendary coloring to the story. Gildas appears as a court physician, Gareth "the minstrel" is mentioned, and Igraine has a serving wench named Isolde. The Grail even appears briefly. A water pageant to celebrate a victory over the heathen includes "a great galley in red and white [which] bore Joseph of Aramathy and the Holy Grail."[5] (Were there clowns and acrobats too?) In spite of a fairly swift plot, Deeping's novel makes hard reading. His language is so overdressed and its re-creation of early Britain so capricious that one has no real sense of either land or people. Nominally the characters are Celts; actually they are the stereotypes of historical romance.

Deeping's *The Man on the White Horse,* though published thirty-two years after *Uther and Ingraine,* marks no advance in the use of Celtic Britain. The hero, Geraint of the White Tower, who according to the author, flourished about 430–450, has an Arthurian name, but he does not resemble the Celtic Geraint at all; nor is Guinevra, whom he rescues from evil Bishop Balthasar of Calleva, intended to be Queen Guinevere. Some of Geraint's friends have Arthurian names — Gawaine, Balan, and Gareth — but beyond this, resemblance ceases. As in *Uther and Igraine,* the setting of the story in Celtic Britain seems an artificial device. The characters act like chivalric knights rather than ancient Celts or Romans.

Arthur himself comes close to appearing in Deeping's novel *The Man Who Went Back.* Here the author changes direction by modernizing his story somewhat. The change is not an improvement. John Hallard, a young English engineer, is thrown back from the present time to fifth-century Britain after being injured in an automobile accident. Here he wins appointment as a "Dux" from Aurelius Superbus, brother of Aurelius Ambrosius, and fights successfully against the Anglo-Saxons. Finally he returns to his own world and readjusts to former ways.

Though Arthur hovers just over the horizon in victories yet to come, Deeping refers to him several times, and in such a confused way that the reader wonders whether he is Nennius' Chieftain or Malory's King. Deeping cannot abandon the medieval Arthur. Though he is called "a certain hero named Arturus... a British dux... who drove the Picts and Scots back into Caledonia, and the Saxons into the sea," this remark is immediately followed by a romantic suggestion: "A band of splendid knights followed him."[6] In an interview with Aurelius Superbus, Hallard muses on the legend in medieval terms:

Aurelius, Ambrosius, Uther, Arthur, Guinivere, Geraint, Modred, Galahad, Tristan and Iseult. Had I been translated into Mallory [sic]? [Then follows a swing-back to the *dux bellorum*.] Was I, perhaps, to ride in arms like one of Arthur's men, that Romano-British Arturus?[7]

This confusion of Arthur's two worlds runs through the whole novel. Hallard dreams of the old legend, wondering if Britain is Christian: "What of Joseph of Arimathea... and the Holy Grail?" He is disturbed in trying to reconcile the shabby realism of London with the glory of the romances: "Was the Arthur Legend compatible with this little cosmos of Commercialists?" As a result of this ambivalence Deeping gives one neither the grandeur of the Middle Ages nor the simplicity of early Britain. The disadvantages of teetering between two worlds are increased by the superficiality of the hero. Deeping never decides whether he shall be an agent of straightaway adventure or a commentator on past and present. As the latter he anticipates passages in John Masefield's *Badon Parchments* in suggesting on one occasion that ancient Saxon and Nazi German are similar, but it is simply a remark in passing and does not have the importance to the story that Masefield gives it. Most of the time Hallard is a bewildered, querulous, and shallow observer, given to peevish outbursts often decorated with modern slang. Yet with all his faults Deeping deserves to be mentioned, for he groped toward a new treatment of Arthur.

In *The Altar of the Legion* (1926) two American authors, Farnham Bishop and Professor Arthur Gilchrist Brodeur, far surpass earlier novelists in dealing with ancient Britain. A story written for young readers, it will please their elders also, for it moves well. Shortly after the death of King Arthur (Bishop and Brodeur make him a king rather than a chieftain) the Romanized Briton Marcianus Drusus commands the last stronghold of Roman power in Britain, the great fortress Castellum Maris at the very southwest tip of England. Here was the lost land of Lyonesse, "Legionis Asa." From this base Drusus leads his troops to the aid of Owain ap Urien, King of North Wales, sorely beset by the Saxons. Much campaigning ensues, and much intrigue touching the Princess Gwenlian, Owain's daughter. Finally, at the very climax of a battle against the Saxons in the streets of Bellerium, hard by Castellum Maris, the peninsula of Lyonesse is swallowed up by an earthquake and tidal wave, leaving only Drusus, his beloved Gwenlian, and about two hundred survivors.

The importance of *The Altar of the Legion* lies in its effective use of the lost land of Lyonesse; its moderately successful attempt to give some of the actuality of life in early Britain; and, most important of all, its respect for the memory of Arthur's greatness as a warrior. The authors take pains to do him honor. While the long poem which ends the Foreword stresses the romantic rather than the "realistic" aspects of Arthur's career, with its reference to his "bannered lords" and his sleep on "the sunken isle of Avalon," earlier in this same section we read of one "schooled in the Roman squadrons, a prince of battles [who] rose in Britain to repel the invader: Arthur the King, greatest among many great and valiant British chiefs." The old King, Owain ap Urien, once the strongest of Arthur's knights, remembers his campaigns of forty years before with Arthur against the Saxons; and his son, Meriaduc, tells how Arthur's few men, trained as heavy cavalry, broke the Saxon shield walls, until his best squadrons were destroyed in the last great battle. Drusus inherits the heroic past. His father had fought under the British liberator and he himself and his troops were welcomed in triumph at Bellerium as "the first Romans to face the Saxon since King Arthur's great, last battle."[8] Bishop and Brodeur's novel, therefore, emphasizes sixth-century rather than medieval chivalric warfare, and the resounding fame of Arthur as a leader. It comes closer than any previous work to suggesting the presence of the *dux bellorum.*[9]

Yet Arthur never appears in the story! In W. Barnard Faraday's novel *Pendragon,* however, he becomes not only the central figure in the tale but also war-leader rather than king and very much a Celt.

Pendragon was the most serious and successful attempt up to that time to suggest the actuality of Arthur and his day. In this field, of course, the storyteller has great leeway for invention, since accurate records of the time are practically nonexistent. R. H. Hodgkin, writing of mid-fifth-century Britain, said "we are facing a dark tract of history which can never — not even with the help of archaeology — be made clear."[10] Yet like all who have introduced Arthur as the Celtic war-leader, Faraday has two fundamental assumptions on which to base his story: (1) the internecine struggle among

90

the peoples of sixth-century Britain, and (2) the sensational successes of a Celtic leader against the *foreign* invaders. In his use of both these assumptions Faraday was almost certainly indebted to Nennius' *Historia Britonum*.

Pendragon describes striking episodes in the career of the Romanized Briton, Artorius, a duke and general serving under King Aurelian of Loegria, a kingdom comprising most of central and southern Britain. He defeats the Picts and Saxons at the Northern Wall and becomes embroiled in the internal struggles of the British kings, particularly as they are stirred up by Guitolin of Dynevawr,[11] a collaborator with the Anglo-Saxons. The situation is eased temporarily by the defeat of Guitolin and by Artorius' growing attachment for Guitolin's niece, the Princess Gwendaello. Finally, when he saves her from assassination by her uncle she is so grateful that she promises him military help. Her forces join his in the last extremity at Badon Hill. Together they inflict a crushing defeat on the Anglo-Saxon invaders, and their love is brought to fruition.

As revealed in his own words and actions,[12] Artorius is the sort of man around whom legends would grow. Of an old British noble house, he had been educated as a Roman citizen, and had served in the Emperor's armies both at home and abroad. He has the efficient outlook of the professional soldier.

I am no fire-eater [he says], and have never yet met a soldier who was, and who was at the same time good at his trade. Still, needs must, and my motto has always been to fight as well as I can, when I must, and no oftener.[13]

He is no "gentil, parfit knyght"; his view of warfare is a quite realistic one. Saxons he hated more than anything else in the world and he believed in exterminating them. With the Christian doctrine of sparing one's enemies he could not agree (he was not a Christian himself). He says bluntly that "the doctrine of sparing enemies was first advanced by those who were acquainted with neither Picts nor Saxons."[14] Yet though he is a cold-blooded fighting man, not at all above spearing two thousand wounded Saxons and Picts and crucifying another two hundred after the fight at Celidon, we do not always think badly of him. If he is harsh to Gwendaello at first, and even if he falls in for a time with a plan to remove her from power in Dynevawr, he had ample reason to do so, considering the swarm of suspicions that rose from plot and counterplot within Britain. What strikes us most about this Arthur is his single-mindedness. He kills Saxons and Picts because there is no survival for his civilization without it; he discards his wavering attitude toward Gwendaello by supporting her fully as soon as he is convinced that it is in the national interest. In short, he is the confident man of action, direct and flexible in mind, unharassed by qualms as to his aims and methods, yet also a man who wins devotion by his patriotic aims and by his undoubted mastery.

Artorius' world is far from that of the medieval romances. Gone are the supernatural marvels of Malory; gone are the noble castles and the glittering banquet halls. There is no attempt to show Britain as better than it was: life was crude and primitive at best, and the British soldiers camped by the ditch of the Northern Wall, watching the bodies of men and horses rotting in the water, had every reason to argue whether a Pict or a Saxon smelt worse when he was dead than when he was alive. Gone are the Holy Grail, and the Round Table.[15] Though the word *knight* is used several times for one of Artorius' followers, only two of Arthur's usual entourage appear: Cador as his lieutenant at the Battle of Celidon and Kai as the seneschal of Gwendaello's court — both of them ancient figures in Welsh legend. The sage and magician Merlin appears as the Welsh prophet Merddin, Chancellor at the court of Maelgwyn of Gwynnedd and chief of the Bards of Mona. Though he has no supernatural powers, he resembles the usual Merlin in being the counselor to royalty,[16] wise beyond all other men. The cleric Gildas also appears, perhaps in an ironic redressing of wrong when, by what Malory might call an "awk stroke," he omitted to mention Arthur in his sixth-century chronicle, *De Excidio et Conquestu Britanniae*. Gildas is a Christian gadfly throughout. Although his fulminations ring no less in Artorius' ears than in those of the Picts and Saxons, it is Artorius' cause which he serves (perhaps as the lesser of the two evils), though daring, ingenious help at the battle of Celidon, and later when Artorius comes to grips with Guitolin.

Whether or not *Pendragon* directly influenced later writers, there can be no question that it set a new pattern for tales of Arthur. This pattern implies describing him as a general rather than a king, as a Celt rather than a Norman noble, as a man rather than an idealized monarch. It implies also a far greater care as to historical background than has been customary in Arthurian tales. Faraday is obviously well-read in the scanty historical records and in the legendary literature of early Britain. His account of the struggles between shadowy kingdoms, his acquaintance with the story of Niall of the Nine Hostages, his use of excerpts from bardic poetry all indicate a desire to make Arthur a real man rather than a symbol or a moral situation.[17] This desire is further carried out by direct and simple realism in describing the mores of the Britons.

The new pattern established by Faraday implies that the raw material of the legend has its own value as fiction, even apart from what Arthur later became. In this new primitivism, poles apart from the eighteenth-century glorification of barbaric or bucolic ways, we observe the few tiny seeds from which flowered the garden of Camelot: the existence of a historical Arthur, a follower or two who bears a name later well known, a sage named Merlin, a primitive circular seating arrangement — perhaps other similar details. Within this pattern is told a story of military and political action, ending either with a famous victory over the heathen or the death of Arthur himself in battle.

Faraday's novel was a good beginning in the new style. Though it does not equal two stories which appeared later (it has neither the historical scope nor the tragic overtones of Frankland's *Bear of Britain*, nor the narrative simplicity of Masefield's *Badon Parchments*); though at times the love story of Artorius and Gwendaello suggests the artificial conventions of earlier tales, its direct approach and its picture of a real war-leader acting in a realistic setting place it well above its predecessors.

In 1944, *The Bear of Britain*, a novel by Edward P. Frankland, continued the method of *Pendragon*. The son of Professor Percy Frankland, a Fellow of the Royal Society, Frankland turned to writing as a career after ill-health caused him to resign his Lectureship in Chemistry at Birmingham University. Arthurian stories gripped him in early boyhood. He remembers, for example, being "rationed" in his retelling of the tales while on walks with his father — "until we reach that tree" — and how he was "absolutely fascinated" by the Norman ruin known as Pendragon Castle in Westmorland. Visits to Tintagel also fired his imagination. At the age of ten he wrote a *Ravenstonedale Book*, "based chiefly on Geoffrey of Monmouth and illustrated with horrible battle pictures of Arthur's victories." Fervid love of the legend lay behind his novel.[18]

More strongly than anyone before him Frankland is convinced that Celtic Arthur and his age deserve to be remembered as they really may have been. Like Faraday, he follows the suggestion of historians that Arthur (known in the novel by a British nickname, the "Bear") was probably of Romano-Celtic stock, and a soldier rather than a king. Both as a person and as a war-leader, Arthur is described much more fully than in *Pendragon,* which dealt only with a few years in Artorius' life and ended with the victory at Badon Hill. *The Bear of Britain* traces his career from his rise to power to final disaster in the Battle of Camlann. Even though Frankland returns to what might be considered the romantic past, his aim is realistic. As he says in the Afterword, his book deals not with "the colourful medieval tapestry of Malory nor the gentlemanly Victorian décor of Tennyson, but a grim and bloodstained pageant of the darkest age in our island's history."

A brief outline of the story will help to keep the general pattern in mind. After Uther Pendragon, "Guletic" (i.e. Prince) of Britain, is poisoned by his son Modron, his other son, Arthur, succeeds him, largely through the persuasive arguments of Modron's incestuous son, Medraut.[19] The rest of the book describes the entanglements and the baffling difficulties of Arthur's career, both public and private. His twelve great victories over his enemies (the same enumerated by Nennius) are won against increasing pressure from enemies without and within. His marriage to Gwenhyvar, daughter of Gwythyr of Strathclyde, gradually falls into a bleak forgetfulness, and his nephew Medraut, his first unwavering supporter, becomes convinced that he must look to his own destiny, in the face of Arthur's inevitable overthrow at the hands of the Saxons. Having tried in vain to unite the chiefs of western Britain in one last effort against the invaders, Arthur goes into a voluntary exile of some years in Brittany. At last he is summoned back to England by the news that Medraut has usurped both wife and kingdom. The Battle of Camlann is the end.

Frankland makes even more use than Faraday of the archaic material at the heart of the legend.[20] Nennius' twelve battles, some of which are described in vivid detail, are the ladder of Arthur's ascent to power. And there are other reflections of primitive Celtic traditions: one catches a hint of the early Tristram-Isolt story when one reads of March (Mark) of Cornwall, who married a young wife and killed his son Drystan in a fit of jealously. As in Faraday, the Round Table appears in a crude, early form. Arthur solves a dispute among his followers as to who shall have the place nearest him by telling them to sit in a circle on the heath "here in this round space that likens a table."[21] The name of Arthur's wife, Gwenhyvar, moreover, is practically the same as that found in the Welsh *Triads*, and the traditional villain Mordred appears under the name Medraut, as in the *Annales Cambriae*. Arthur's nickname as the "Bear" may have been suggested by the person Gildas so designates in Chapter 32 of his *Excidio*.[22] Finally, Frankland introduces an incident based upon an almost forgotten reference in the section of Nennius' *Historia* called "De Mirabilibus Britanniae," when he tells the story of the young man Anir who is unwittingly slain by his father Arthur.

The battle scenes in *The Bear of Britain* are full, swift, and dramatic, and one follows eagerly as Arthur's host scales the Pictish castle of Bregion, or flings itself in one last desperate assault against the Saxons on Badon Hill, or dissolves into broken fragments at Camlann under the cries of Medraut's force, "Hew the Welshmen!" Battle in sixth-century Britain was not a chivalric encounter of knights on horseback but rather the brutal cut and thrust, the savage infighting of men who had marched all day and who fought under the law of kill or be killed, not under the code of medieval combat. Though of course it is impossible to say how close Frankland comes to literal truth, it is certain that his accounts of fighting sweep one along. There is no attempt to turn war into a ceremonial pageant. Quite the reverse: war is a grim, brutalizing business; agony and death ride with it; rapine, fear, and starvation follow in its train. Even the fruits of victory seem illusory.

It is this shadowing sense of hopelessness which intensifies the conflict in *The Bear of Britain*. An air of doom hovers over the book, not unlike the sense of disaster which grows more and more powerful in the *Morte Darthur*. Arthur himself is greatly gifted: he has the farseeing eye of the great Captain and a driving will. Yet the odds are too heavy against him. Early in the story, after seven striking victories in the North, he wonders if he can do as well in the South. In the long run he cannot. The strain of trying to unite fractious British rulers against the invader, and finally the defection of Medraut, prove to be more than even he can endure.

The relationship of Arthur, Gwenhyvar, and Medraut is charged with disaster. To Gwenhyvar, shortly after her marriage, Arthur was so "godlike" that she felt frighteningly insufficient in his presence. Yet — and here one begins to see the flaw — he did not have the Jovian moral aloofness of Tennyson's Arthur. As he and Gwenhyvar drifted more and more apart one began to learn of Arthur's lapses: even before his marriage there had been Garwen and Gwyll, mothers of his bastard sons Lacheu and Anir,[23] and in the dark days after his great victories there had been the harlot Indec. Medraut of the quick wit, the easy address, and the flame of poetic song was gradually to turn this erratic fumbling with women to his advantage. Quite early he decides that he would like

97

to marry Gwenhyvar, rather than see her mated with a demigod. In such an apparently stock situation it is to Frankland's credit that Medraut acts like a human being and not simply like the conventional villain he is usually made to be. His is no impulsive act to catch the tide of the moment; he undergoes a gradual change over a number of years through his increasing conviction that Arthur is fighting a hopeless battle both against his countrymen and the invaders. To this is added a dark and unscrupulous opportunism in his own nature and a suggestion of satanic dedication. After the great victories in the North, when he falls into gloomy prophecy of disaster, Arthur says to him "your powers come of evil."[24] And later, when he feels at one with Gwenhyvar, he speaks to her with almost ghoulish satisfaction of his unnatural birth, and, in revealing his sinister plans, maintains that "wherever we look in this land . . . the weapons of hell outmatch those of heaven."[25]

Arthur comes to his end at Camlann through forces both within and without which he could not control. Yet he goes down with stout heart, and with compassion for his misguided and suffering countrymen. The spectacle of Briton fighting Briton in the last great battle causes him such anguish that he hurls his sword Caledvulch into the river Brue. With a borrowed weapon he cleaves Medraut's skull, and receives his death wound. His Avalon is no misty island of forgetfulness. Garwen and Bedwyr bear him into a hollow hill, and, sealing the entrance with turf, leave him sleeping in a place forever unknown.

The faint similarities to Malory and Tennyson in this last episode are evident enough. Yet *The Bear of Britain* takes place in another world, a world stripped alike of medieval splendor and of allegory. In the Foreword to the novel, David Lloyd George says that the author has cleared away "the lum-

ber of incredible mediaeval fantasies under which the personality of [Arthur] has been buried for centuries." Leaving out
of account the slighting reference to the riches of medieval
romance, this statement accentuates Frankland's achievement.
Though his novel has defects — among them conversation
which is sometimes stilted and a cramping confinement of
Arthur's long career within 250 pages — it stays in the mind
long after reading. John Masefield's *Badon Parchments* sur-
passes it in continuous narrative skill but not in the total impression it leaves. For even in brief compass *The Bear of
Britain* makes us sharply aware of Britain's agony and of
destructive forces against which Arthur hurls himself, at last
in vain. Treachery and disillusionment dog the Bear's foot-
steps, yet his purpose holds even in the face of engulfing disaster, and after we lay the book aside there emerges the living
form of a new Arthur, a man who may have been very like
the *dux bellorum* of the Britons, a man cast in the heroic mold,
around whom rich legends of chivalric adventure might well
gather.

John Masefield, whose *Badon Parchments* (1947) is one of
the most recent accounts of Arthur as the *dux bellorum*, felt
the Celtic influence early in life, particularly through reading
the *Mabinogion* and "Fiona Macleod." "I began to see ... [he
writes] that the Celts ... were protesting, by their delicacy and
elegance, against the great, sprawling, hideous, filthy apathy of
a commercial age."[26] This interest has led Masefield to use
much Celtic material in his Arthurian stories, particularly his
play *Tristan and Isolt,* and *Midsummer Night.* Though in the
latter Arthur is definitely a king, there are touches which show
that Masefield tried to give freshness to the traditional material. "The Begetting of Arthur," for example, makes Uther a
Roman Briton, pleading for the help of King Merchyon of

Cornwall against the heathen. The poem describing the Battle of Badon Hill is a curious mixture of old and new. For while most of the story is quasi-historical, in the Saxon leader Loki's expedition to find the fat English herds discovered years before by his grandfather and in the battle with Arthur which ensues, we read that Lancelot, Hector, and Gawaine are by the side of the British king! Gwenivach, sister of Guinevere and a figure in the Welsh *Triads,* appears as one of the members of Arthur's petrified court within the hill in the title poem, "Midsummer Night," as well as in "Gwenivach Tells." Also in "Midsummer Night" there is mention of that little-known young man Lacheu, here described as the son of Lancelot and Guinevere, and not (as in the ancient Welsh poems) the son of Arthur. And the account of Arthur's last battle in *Midsummer Night* is much more direct and realistic than usual. Chivalric heroism is subordinated to realistic violence. It is also worth noting that Modred is allied with a northern pirate, Kolgrim.

In *Badon Parchments* Masefield completely abandons medieval tradition in describing how Arthur may have acted as a Celtic general. The story unfolds in a report of events in Britain made to the Emperor Justinian and the Empress Theodora by their envoy, John of Cos, on his return to Byzantium. At the outset, Arthur, a British soldier of royal blood, has just arrived from Byzantium at the court of King Aurelian in southern Britain. He is told that during his two years' absence his friends in the government have been driven from power, and that there is great unrest in the southern realm. "We were made to feel [says John of Cos] that Aurelian rules no Kingdom, but holds together a loose confederacy of jealous little kings."[27] This internal confusion is greatly aggravated by imminent danger of war with the Anglo-Saxons. King Pedda of

the "Black Heathen" to the west of Aurelian's kingdom, in-
cited by a ruthless adviser called The Burner and fortified by
trumped-up charges of outrages by the Britons, is preparing
to attack. With him are allied King Osla, a renegade Briton,
and Ceretig, a Gaulish pirate. On finding that his views on
warfare are not well received by Aurelian's advisers, Arthur
goes to the help of King Ocvran in the North and speedily
disperses the Heathen in his kingdom. Meantime war breaks
out in the South. Aurelian is beset by hordes of Saxons and
Gaulish pirates. His forces, under young Prince Cador, stand
at a collection of buildings called "The Springs," and, having
beaten off all attacks, move to the offensive against the strong
Saxon position on Badon Hill. There they are on the brink of
defeat when Arthur arrives with a force of Welsh mounted
archers to turn the tide. Pedda, Osla, and Ceretig are killed;
shortly after the battle The Burner takes poison to avoid
hanging. So, as John of Cos says:

The Black Heathen power is broken. The Outlanders every-
where have submitted to the Britons with all the servility they
ever show in defeat. The pirates settled in Gaul will raid no
more for many years to come. The Heathen in northern Europe
will hardly again venture to Britain for booty as in the past.[28]

Badon Parchments, unlike *Pendragon* and *The Bear of Britain,* stresses the political and military aspects of the situation
in Britain, rather than Arthur as a central character. Modern
readers will appreciate Masefield's skill in drawing parallels
between the campaign of the sixth century and the war against
Nazi Germany. The Heathen anticipated Hitler's methods by
some fourteen hundred years: Fifth Columnists in the guise of
friendly young visitors had done their work before the attack;
manufactured incidents justified the assault on the Britons.
Even Hitler's statement at Munich that he had no more terri-

torial claims in Europe is paralleled by King Pedda's lulling assertion to Aurelian, before hostilities break out, that "he has no desire whatsoever for more land than his own kingdom."[29] The Saxons were Ur-Nazis: "They hear no truth from infancy. They are ordered to believe just as they are ordered to do. They neither disobey nor disbelieve."[30] Like the "Herrenvolk," the Heathen are "the Elect of God, the Chosen of Heaven," and in one instance the underlings of The Burner actually give a prototypal Nazi salute:

As [The Burner] ceased speaking, there was a pause while one might have counted three, then the right hands of the three men shot upwards; all three men shouted, "Ha," and slapped their hearts a sounding smack as they brought their hands downwards. It was the Heathen salute; it was very smartly done, and though it was done by The Burner to King Pedda or himself and by his underlings to The Burner, the Britons present supposed that it was done to Aurelian and thought that it was a fine tribute.[31]

In other ways also *Badon Parchments* is a commentary on government under stress. We learn early that Arthur's friends have fallen from official grace in his absence, and this has important effects for him, for it means that he is shunted off onto the northern campaign rather than being immediately appointed to command under Aurelian. Further, the first third of the book is taken up with the Council called at Aurelian's capital to discuss ways of meeting the threatened war. There is shrewd satire here. To a Britain which has recently emerged by the skin of its teeth from a war all but lost, the statement of the Prefect for War is very much to the point:

In the clamour, an elegant little man, in a scarlet cloak, splendid with gold, and a face which reminded one of an earthworm . . . rose to say that, "Though it is not in the public interest to declare what has been done and is being done to put the defences of the Kingdom upon a war-footing, yet I can assure all present that any enemy . . . will meet with an extremely warm reception. Our preparedness was never greater; our people may sleep securely in their beds."[32]

In the light of later muddle and disaster, redeemed only at the last moment by Arthur's arrival, and in the light of the angry words spoken by Britons of our own time, such a passage as this strikes home swiftly and well. Also to the point, as we remember France's collapse in the late war, is the scene in which Aurelian's ministers consider capitulating to the Saxons.

Though Masefield's Arthur is not the central character he is in *The Bear of Britain* and *Pendragon*, he is still a striking person. Not tormented like Frankland's Arthur, he is no less gifted. His analysis of political and military difficulties is sure; his training in the Imperial army had convinced him of the need for mobile troops — mounted archers — and if his suggestions received short shrift at first, they were spectacularly vindicated at Badon Hill.[33] To his strategic insight is added not only the old campaigner's quiet confidence but also a moral fire which infected his troops. This is how he explains to Aurelian his plan of organizing his soldiers into bands of "Chosen Brotherhood":

My hope would be for rather small parties, not more than fifty, each pledged to a particular Captain, each sworn to support the general cause, and the chosen general leader. It would be the aim of every leader of fifty to make the membership of his fifty a distinction. The spirit in the army of the Holy City is not so much a military spirit, as the spirit of religion; the men consecrate themselves to a cause, because they love the cause, and know that faith supports it.[34]

In his address when he takes command of the troops of King Ocvran there is a long passage filled with the moral and religious dedication of a Christian Arthur. He ends thus:

Sometimes, you may have heard men speak of Christians as "children of God." Think of this when you ride out. You, if you are children of God, will be doing your Father's business, of justice or wisdom, of righteousness, of truth, of light of every kind.[35]

The young men of King Ocvran followed his lead eagerly. Groups of fifties, called Tables, were organized; the best of them all, Arthur's own, was the Round Table. (Here Masefield suggests Malory rather than primitive Celtic tradition.) In this episode and indeed throughout, Arthur acts with a kind of youthful assurance and serenity. At Aurelian's Council King Ocvran speaks of him as "a young man whose face is that of happy fortune." His strength touches the stricken land of Britain.

Badon Parchments shows Masefield's mastery of swift narrative. The story is well integrated, the long deliberations of the Council leading, after a short interlude sketching Arthur's activities in the north, to the invasion of Aurelian's kingdom. Though it is a novel of only 151 pages it seems neither hasty nor rawboned, for Masefield has a sense of pace and an eye for striking detail. Even in the deliberations of the Council the story moves with a sure, masculine stride; character after character is struck off in a happy phrase, and by alternation and suspense the arguments lead to a fitting climax. And when he brings you to the battlefield, Masefield is surpassingly good. It would be hard to imagine a more vivid re-creation of the fury of savage combat: masses of Saxons hurl themselves on the palisades of "The Springs" and hew a small breach through the timbers, only to be engulfed in a whirling melee, and the Britons again and again move up the slopes of Badon Hill, to come to a crunching halt against the Saxon wedges. The feel of battle is there, when an accident like one shot from a Saxon catapult can affect the whole course of an attack, or when the trumpets of Arthur's mounted archers and the first flight of arrows can break the Saxon resistance almost instantaneously. And the feel of battle is not only in the brutal clash of assault; it is in the magnificent assurance of the individual soldier as well:

I saw one bowman who stood near a willow-stump with his boy-attendant. The bowman was famous, I was told. The boy had placed some twenty arrows point-downwards in the earth to the right of the archer; his duty was to pluck up arrow after arrow and present it instantly to the bowman so that he could nock it and shoot with the least possible delay. This man and boy were the coolest creatures I have ever seen. They stood their ground, shooting down man after man, till it seemed that they must be engulfed. Then, just as we thought them lost, the boy plucked up the remaining arrows and slipped away to the side, the bowman sent a shaft through the nearest Heathen and slipped away to the other side, and in another instant they were safe, and again shooting, and then again slipping away.[36]

Stripped down to its "historic" essentials, then, and concentrated upon the great climactic campaign, Masefield's story of the *dux bellorum* makes very good reading. Here again Arthur emerges as a man whom legend could not possibly overlook. And the fact that medieval romance turned him into someone he never was does not for a moment dim his lustre as the man he may have been.

Very recently another novelist has followed Masefield's

lead in describing the battle of Badon Hill. Alfred Duggan's *Conscience of the King* (1951) chronicles the long and opportunistic career of Cerdic, King of the West Saxons. During an expedition against the Demetians and Dumnonians begun in the year 515, Cerdic hears stories of a new "Roman" (that is, British) leader who has had striking success in the North. This leader, a man named Artorius (he was also known to the Celts as "the Bear", which is "Art" in their tongue), had apparently studied military science at Rome, and was reported to make very successful use of cavalry. Cerdic discovers this to his pain when he is surprised by Artorius' forces at Badon Hill in the year 516. The cavalrymen were modelled after the Roman cataphractarii, mounted on heavy horses and completely armored. They bore lances and long, heavy swords. Cerdic's force is decimated in the fight, and though a remnant eventually escapes, Artorius' victory is a resounding one.

Artorius does not figure as a character in the story at all, yet Duggan makes such interesting use of primitive material, especially in suggesting ways of bridging the gap between the *dux bellorum* and the medieval monarch, that his novel deserves to be read and remembered. First, there is the suggestion already familiar, that the Celtic Arthur employed heavy cavalry. Duggan is more explicit in describing the appearance and equipment of this force than earlier writers and he also suggests plausible reasons for Arthur's eventual defeat. Cerdic shrewdly improvises means of dealing with the cavalry in escaping from the trap at Badon Hill. He charges Artorius' position at the foot of the hill and posts his men in clumps about the large leather and canvas pavilions (reminiscent of the medieval romancers) where the horsemen cannot get at them easily, and where the mounts can be put out of action by hamstringing. Further, Cerdic reflects on the difficulty

Artorius would have in finding new horses, for his mounts were not the small British breed but were obviously big, heavy animals imported from the continent. In the second place, Duggan gives forward-looking hints of Artorius' later career. According to reports which had reached Cerdic, Artorius' first devoted followers, who were sworn, like him, to the task of freeing Britain, were gradually supplanted by others less high-minded. Eventually one of his captains rebelled against him, and rumor even had it that he was the lover of Artorius' wife. In time the body of heavy cavalry disintegrated. There was much fighting, and after a defeat Artorius went into hiding. The common folk among the Britons, says Cerdic, still hope that he will come from his hiding place one day to lead them against their enemies.

Conscience of the King is a simple, realistic story which makes skillful use of scraps of legendary and historical material and the invention of the novelist. Though the campaigns of the *dux bellorum* play a minor part in the story, they do so convincingly both as history and narrative.

The re-creators of Arthur as the *dux bellorum* deserve to be remembered, for they are responsible for one of the most original innovations in the history of the cycle. They have shown more than the amateur's familiarity with the scanty and confusing early records of Arthur, particularly Gildas, Nennius, and ancient Welsh poetry, and they have reconstructed the story of Arthur's exploits from the sparse material with fresh and lively invention. With the groundwork thus laid, perhaps one day high tragic poetry will chronicle the war-leader of the Celts.[37]

FIVE

The Comedy of Camelot

As the legend grew more and more popular in the nineteenth and twentieth centuries writers began to try experiments in parody and satire. The wide gulf between the Middle Ages and the Machine Age made comic versions almost inevitable. Also, those who knew the legend realized that the knights were not always deadly solemn, any more than they were exclusively concerned with what Roger Ascham attacked as "open manslaughter and bold bawdry." The comic moments in Malory are often overlooked. There is the riotous practical joke played on cowardly King Mark, for example, when Sir Dagonet (King Arthur's fool) disguises himself in Launcelot's armor and sends Mark scuttling off in a panic, at which "the knyghtes rode here and there cryenge and chacyng after kynge Marke that all the forest range of the noyse." Also it would be hard to forget the dry answer of the Lady of the Lake, who by magic causes the vacillating, tiresome Sir Pelleas to hate the Lady Ettarde who had treated him so scurvily. "'And now such grace God hath sent me [says Pelleas] that I hate hir as much as I have loved hir.' 'Thanke me therefore,' seyde the Lady of the Lake." Even the peerless Launcelot plays a comic bit, and in it Malory takes a dig at the "modern woman" who doesn't know her place. While resting in a forest he has the bad luck to be wounded by a lady archer who aimed at a hind and hit instead a be-hind — his own. "Lady, or damesell, whatsomever ye be, in an evyll tyme bare ye thys bowe. The devyll made you a shoter."

Before the nineteenth century, however, comic treatment of the legend is very rare. About the only earlier piece still remembered is Fielding's play *Tom Thumb* (1730), the scene of which is laid in what is supposed to be King Arthur's court. In the nineteenth century there was a marked increase. John Hookham Frere's *The Monks and the Giants* (1817–1818) and Thomas Love Peacock's *The Misfortunes of Elphin* (1829) — both good comedy and the latter one of the best in the field — reflected renewed interest in the legend during the early part of the century. (The *Morte Darthur* was reprinted three times in 1816 and 1817.) The publication of Tennyson's *Idylls* also set the wags to work. General Edward Hamley's "Sir Tray: An Arthurian Idyl," *Blackwood's Magazine* (January, 1873), burlesques the later life of the Lady of Shalott, and George Du Maurier's *A Legend of Camelot* (1898) pokes fun at both Tennyson and the Pre-Raphaelites. Though this japery was largely confined to England, America soon joined the sport. Mark Twain's *A Connecticut Yankee in King Arthur's Court* (1889), ostensibly a piece of serious social analysis as well as a hilarious spoof on the days of chivalry, has been popular — and tremendously so — for its comedy rather than its bitter attack on the Middle Ages.

Humorous versions of the legend have increased in the twentieth century, but they are mostly far inferior to *A Connecticut Yankee* and *The Misfortunes of Elphin*. Only in T. H.

White's novels, especially *The Sword in the Stone,* do we find long-sustained, first-rate comedy. Nearly all the versions before Mr. White's are brief *jeux d'esprit,* gaily tossed off by writers well-known in other fields. They are generally set in Arthur's time,[1] and delight in ridiculing chivalric love and warlike adventure. A number of them are slight satiric poems, depending often on verbal humor — wrenched medieval language, modern slang, and the like. Examples of this rather feeble wit can be found in Don Marquis' "Tristram and Isolt" and "Lancelot and Guinevere" and Christopher Ward's series of burlesques on various Arthurian characters — this last being the best of the lot.[2]

Much more ambitious and generally more successful is Charlton Miner Lewis' *Gawayne and the Green Knight* (1904), a full-length, waggish retelling of the familiar story. In his introductory verses the author describes his poem as "A plain, straightforward man's unvarnished word, / Part sad, part sweet, — and part of it absurd." The plot follows the original closely, except for the added figure of the Lady Elfinhart as Gawayne's sweetheart. On the whole it is not a bad piece, for Lewis has a fairly good comic sense in pointing up the incongruity between past and present. For example, when the Green Knight's head is cut off, green blood gushes forth like "a flood of crème de menthe!" and the shout that follows is like "the long cheers [that] roll / Cacophonous, for him who kicks a goal."[3]

There are at least two short stories also that develop comedy more fully and successfully than the brief poems mentioned earlier. One of the episodes in Booth Tarkington's *Penrod* (1914) tells how the boy Penrod Schofield is dragooned into taking the part of the "Child Sir Lancelot" in "The Pageant of the Table Round," written by Mrs. Lora

Rewbush and presented for the benefit of the Coloured Infants' Betterment Society in a midwestern town. Penrod shows the standard boyish reaction to all this nonsense and approaches the ordeal with dread, especially when he discovers the costume his mother and sister have concocted. In desperation he hits on an inspired idea. When the "Child King Arthur" calls on the knights to doff their mantles preparatory to being knighted, Penrod is revealed in a pair of baggy blue overalls, which he had found in the janitor's room just before going on stage. The audience is vastly amused, and so is the reader, for Tarkington knows boys, and the anguish they can suffer at being made public spectacles in sissified performances. The nauseous doggerel which Mrs. Rewbush had written for her actors was enough to make any self-respecting child writhe.

Heywood Broun's short story, "The Fifty First Dragon," also makes good reading. The piece deals with Gawaine Le Coeur-Hardy, a boy who is a source of considerable worry to the Headmaster and the assistant Professor of Pleasaunce at the "knight school." In despair over Gawaine's poor work in his studies the Headmaster decides to teach him dragon-killing, and gives him a magic word to use in all such battles. At last the boy has found what he can do, and in no time at all runs up forty-nine victories. Then he meets number fifty, a wise old dragon who talks to him so convincingly that he forgets the magic word. When the dragon attacks, however, Gawaine dispatches him with no trouble at all. His puzzlement is increased when the Headmaster tells him that the word had no power whatsoever. The next day he disappears; some time later his friends find pieces of his equipment where a small dragon had been seen.

"The Fifty First Dragon" is neat, brisk foolery. In this story

111

the suffering, lumpish schoolboy takes a place in Arthur's kingdom. Like his modern counterpart he is weak on theory; lectures on the history, anatomy, and habits of dragons confuse him. On the practice field it is a different story. Long after Gawaine's disappearance old alumni of the "knight school" remember the excitement they felt as he charged across the field toward a paper dragon. And the dull boy finally makes good. Broun's last touch in the story is one of the best. The school keeps his memory green by a shield bearing his name and mounted with fifty pairs of dragons' ears. The record was never equalled.

Two other prose tales are especially interesting because they anticipate the highly sophisticated, cynical approach found in the novels of John Erskine and elsewhere. Here the satire is much more worldly, much more smartly "knowing" in the modern sense than in the comic pieces discussed so far. Maurice Baring's "The Camelot Jousts" (in *Dead Letters,* 1910) consists of a series of letters (and their replies) from Guinevere to Arthur, Lancelot, and Iseult just before the time when Lancelot wore Elaine's favor in a tournament. Though they hint at large and troublesome problems, they will be remembered chiefly for their chatty, "modern" manner. The best pair is a feline exchange between Guinevere and Iseult. Arthur wants Iseult invited to the jousts; she seems to be behaving herself and the old scandal about Tristram has died down. Guinevere consents reluctantly and writes a gushing letter. A postscript artfully tells of Tristram's marriage to Iseult the Lilyhanded. The bride was "a dream of beauty" and the groom was "in tearing spirits" though grown rather fat! Iseult replies in kind. Lancelot, she has heard, will not take part in the tournament for fear of being beaten. And is it true that he is engaged to Elaine? She is a lovely person, but (with vinegar in every word) Iseult thought that he never liked young girls! Of its kind Baring's sketch is good. For one thing the author knows when to stop, a point John Erskine could well take to heart.

Baring's sophistication, however, pales before the worldliness about to be described. James Branch Cabell's novel *Jurgen* (1919) introduces Arthurian characters among the inhabitants of the imaginary land of Poictesme, a region as unlike Malory's Britain as can be conceived. The world of the *Morte Darthur,* for all its mythical invention, is one of artless simplicity and candor. You know where you stand in Malory, because chivalric responsibility and moral law support his society, even in the breach. Poictesme, on the other hand, is like Rabelais' Abbey of Thélème, where everyone, including the author, does as he likes. Cabell's novel aims among other things to debunk chivalric romance, yet its manner of doing so is not the usual and obvious one. The book relies on very elaborate irony in expression and situation; it assumes a worldly, formalized satiric tone, leading to ingeniously pedantic disquisitions, the whole underlaid by disillusionment and mockery. Under these conditions, love is a game of erotic excitement played casually, and described with a kind of smirking relish, in elaborate sexual symbolism.

Jurgen created an enormous sensation among American readers when it first appeared. The more the censors belabored it, the more the undergraduates of all ages loved it. To them it was the ultimate word in sophisticated freedom. Thirty-five years after it is hard to recapture that fine, careless frenzy.

The story concerns a middle-aged pawnbroker, Jurgen, who regains his youth by enchantment and sets out to find the fullness of life he had missed before. In the course of his adventures he comes upon Guenevere (the daughter of Gogyrvan,

King of Glathion and the Red Islands) magically asleep in a cave with a villainous looking old King named Thragnar. He awakens her with a kiss and informs her he is the Duke of Logreus. Shortly thereafter he asks Gogyrvan for the hand of his daughter, only to be told that she had already been sought by Arthur. This does not deter Jurgen (nor Guenevere either) from intimate attentions, though out of deference to the advice of Merlin, he refrains from coming to Arthur's court as one of the hundred knights chosen by King Gogyrvan to accompany his gift of the Round Table. He says farewell to Guenevere and consoles himself with the expert charms of Anaïtis, the Lady of the Lake. At the end of the story, after various non-Arthurian adventures, Jurgen again meets Guenevere. Her old world is gone: Lancelot is a monk at Glastonbury, Arthur has been taken to Avalon, and she offers to marry Jurgen, even though he is again a paunchy, middle-aged pawnbroker. But he has done with illusions and they part forever.

Jurgen stands alone in the Arthurian comedy, isolated by Cabell's bizarre inventions of mythology and by oblique, "sophisticated" humor and quasi-intellectual irony. It is sardonic rather than joyful mockery. At its best it does sometimes amuse with its "realistic" attitude toward the world of chivalry, as for example in the account of Jurgen's exploits at a tournament. He overcomes Sir Dodinas le Sauvage, Sir Hector de Maris, and others, only to be unhorsed by Earl Damas of Listenise:

[He] slid contentedly down the tail of his fine horse. His part in the tournament was ended, and he was heartily glad of it.[4]

By and large, however, the antics in Poictesme are more confusing than amusing.

Up to this point the development of Arthurian comedy in

the twentieth century has been rather erratic. With the publication in 1938 of T. H. White's *The Sword in the Stone,* however, the situation improved tremendously. Though White had
begun to attract attention as a writer before he published this
book, in all likelihood he will be remembered best for his
comic treatment of Arthur's Britain.

In a letter to the author (November 28, 1948), Mr. White
briefly sketches his association with the legend:

I first read [the *Morte Darthur*] at the age of 8. At the age of
11 I chose it for a school prize. At Cambridge, where I took
1st class honours in English, I wrote my thesis on it. Twelve
years ago I began to write my own version, and I hope to have
completed it in one more year. There is one more book to
come, called *The Candle in the Wind,* and when all four
books are published together they will be called *The Once
and Future King.*

In a postscript Mr. White adds:

The oldest existing writing of mine about the Arthurian cycle
is a very bad poem on Sir Sagramore, which I wrote at the
age of 16! So you see that quite a slice of my life has been
devoted to the subject.

If the evidence of his three Arthurian novels were not
enough, this letter would make clear that White is not toying
with the legend as a diversion from other matters. It is a major
concern, and his close association with it is strengthened by
scholarly understanding.

The main outline of *The Sword in the Stone* is simple. In
effect it is the story of Arthur's boyhood in the household of
his foster father, Sir Ector of the Forest Sauvage. Merlyn is
his tutor. Under his guidance and in the casual, knockabout
world which he explores with his foster brother Kay, he learns

a great deal — not out of books. The years pass, and Arthur (or Wart, as he is called) attends the great tournament in London as Kay's squire. There he pulls the sword from the stone and succeeds to the throne of his father, Uther Pendragon.

In barest summary *The Sword in the Stone* follows the *Morte Darthur* — yet with what a difference! Though White has a great affection for Malory, he reworks the old story in an entirely fresh and original way. First, he fills in the blank pages of Arthur's boyhood; second, he touches the whole with brilliant comic invention, both in character and situation; finally, through a series of remarkable supernatural transformations he leads the boy Arthur toward the wisdom which he will sorely need as King. It is essential not to overlook this last point, for *The Sword in the Stone* is far from the unmixed buffoonery of most of its predecessors; it is also a serious study of what the governor should learn.

Yet White's serious purpose never gives a lumpish air to the book; in fact one of his major triumphs is the way in which he combines grave and gay in one harmonious whole. Certainly the gay predominates, but never to the exclusion of the fundamental soundness of character which White's people reveal or the wisdom which comes to Arthur in a number of ways. In spite of its extravagance and hilarity, life in *The Sword in the Stone* is firm at the core.

The England that we see — "England of the fifteenth century, or whenever it was," as White says — is a land of happy exploration. Though there are foreshadowings of dark troubles lying in wait for Arthur as King, for the most part it is carefree youth that rules. In keeping with this spirit it is "merry England" that we see: a country where lords and commons live together snugly in an acceptance of their separate stations, where there seem to be no worries economic or political, and where Christmas banquets send song to the rafters. White's originality and his accurate knowledge of medieval life stand him in good stead. The book is enlivened with passages which bring an ancient place or custom before our eyes. It would be hard to imagine a more vivid picture of Ector's Castle than we find in *The Sword in the Stone*. There it is spread out before you, from outer curtain wall and inner keep to the cow byres, the smithy and "my lord's and lady's chambers." Early in the book White describes the Mews, where Ector's hawks are kept. His eye for detail is so extraordinary — the appearance of the room, the equipment, the perches for the birds — and his style is so lucid that we seem to stand there ourselves. It would be hard to match also his description of the great boar hunt in Ector's forest, or his careful account of the technique of jousting or the ceremonies leading to knighthood. Passages like these make us eager companions in Arthur's explorations of an England that is fresh and new.

His companions are picturesque enough to keep any boy on his toes. Here we get the full flavor of White's comedy, a hilarious mixture of ancient and modern England and a satire which is never touched with malice. His people are types but they are much more real than usual: the bluff, gouty Sir Ector cast in the role of the sportin' English squire; his friends Sir Grummore Grummursum and King Pellinore, two knights errant whose monumental inefficiency is mitigated by their "Old School Spirit"; the pouter-pigeon drill sergeant (right out of the pages of *Punch*) who teaches Wart and Kay how to joust ("Nah, nah, Master Kay ... the spear should be 'eld between the thumb and forefinger of the right 'and, with the shield in line with the seam of the trahser leg"); and the petulant, warmhearted Nannie who cares for the two boys.

Several of the characters are played "straight": William Twyti, the King's huntsman who manages the boar hunt in the Forest Sauvage, "a shrivelled, harassed-looking man," an acknowledged master in all that pertained to venery, yet abysmally bored with all of it except the sport of chasing hares; Robin Hood (his companions said his proper name was Wood), the efficient man of action, a forester who knew all the ways of wild and human game; and Wart's constant companion, Kay, a good boy but a little unstable, who tries to conceal his sense of insecurity by throwing his weight around a little.

The magician Merlyn towers over all the other people in the book except Wart himself. Here White's comedy has its broadest scope, for Merlyn's adventures range all the way from waggish tricks of magic (which once in a while fail to come off) to pedagogic transformation of Arthur into various beasts. He is the rather absent-minded, eccentric duffer of our own acquaintance — the man who lives alone in the country, surrounded by a confusion of odd objects which reflect an active and original mind. Like others of this sort he is somewhat untidy, as well he might be when we remember that his pet owl Archimedes (a speaking owl, by the way) roosted on his hair. Wart comes upon his cottage by chance and is invited to visit his upstairs room. It was an amazing place; a stuffed "corkindrill" hung from the rafters, and winked one glass eye at Merlyn as he entered; there were "hundreds of thousands" of brown books which gave out "a smell of solid brownness which was most secure." There were stuffed birds, and a fox's mask, a salmon and a basilisk mounted as sporting trophies. Six grass snakes sported in "a kind of aquarium." Besides all these Wart noticed

a gun-case with all sorts of weapons which would not be invented for half a thousand years, a rod-box ditto, . . . twelve pairs of boots, a dozen purse-nets, three dozen rabbit wires, twelve cork-screws, an ant's nest between two glass plates, ink-bottles of every possible color from red to violet, darning-needles, a gold metal for being the best scholar at Eton, . . . the fourteenth edition of the Encyclopaedia Britannica (marred as it was by the sensationalism of the popular plates), two paint-boxes (one oil, one water color), three globes of the known geographical world, a few fossils, the stuffed head of a camelopard, six pismires, some glass retorts with cauldrons, bunsen burners, etc., and a complete set of cigarette cards depicting wild fowl by Peter Scott.[5]

The man who lived in this astonishing room, however, was no fuddy-duddy hermit; he was the greatest expert in the whole field of magic, white or black. His powers are put to a stern test early in the book, when Arthur and Kay are captured by Madame Mim, a notable practitioner of black magic. (On her garden gate was screwed a brass plate, bearing the following legend: "Madame Mim, B.A. (Dom-Daniel) Pianoforte Needlework Necromancy. No Hawkers, circulars or Income Tax. Beware of the Dragon.") Merlyn arrives in the very nick of time to save the boys, which he does by slaying Madame Mim in the kind of duel magicians used in place of jousting. ("Now we shall see [said Merlyn] what a double-first at Dom-Daniel avails against the private education of my master Bleise.") In the contest each magician turns himself into some animal, vegetable, or mineral which would destroy his opponent. Hecate, wearing an eyeshade, sits on a stepladder as umpire; an ingenious move by Merlyn calls forth "Oh, well played, sir!" from the Wart on the sidelines. At breakneck speed the contestants change into one form or another. Merlyn is hard pressed, and when Madame Mim becomes an aullay, an animal much larger than an elephant (into which Merlyn had turned), the fight seems hopeless. Then Merlyn plays his master stroke:

[He] turned himself successively into the microbes, not yet discovered, of hiccoughs, scarlet fever, mumps, whooping cough, measles and heat spots, and from a complication of all these complaints the infamous Madame Mim had immediately expired.[6]

White's wit is unusually fresh and original. It would be hard to forget the national anthem which brings Sir Ector's Christmas feast to a close:

> *God save King Pendragon,*
> *May his reign long drag on,*
>   *God save the King.*
> *Send him most gorious,*
> *Great and uproarious,*
> *Horrible and hoarious,*
>   *God save our King.*[7]

And Sir Grummore and King Pellinore have blundered their way into the company of Arthur's immortals. To their invincible incompetence is added the wistful pathos of good intentions gone wrong. For all their faults one cannot help liking them. They are eager to perform all knightly devoirs, which they approach with the apprehension of small boys in their first rugger scrum. The description of their joust is a masterpiece of parody, for "the terrible battle," as White calls it, is not the usual set piece of comic incongruities; it is really the blundering fisticuffs of two little boys on the playing field. What began as a genteel, friendly passage at arms on horseback deteriorates into a very unknightly rough-and-tumble afoot, with the two butting at one another like boars, their

tempers growing worse by the minute. Finally after a regret-
table deception when Pellinore says "Pax" and then resumes
fighting the battle moves to a thunderous climax. The champions hurtle together but miss their aim. Grummore rams his
head against a beech; Pellinore hits a chestnut tree. Merlyn
assures Wart that "they'll be the best of friends when they
come to." And so they are from that time on, for they are both
kindly if very limited chevaliers, like the well-disciplined
public-school boy, incapable of nursing grudges. As a matter
of fact, on one occasion Pellinore raises his status as exponent
of the "Old School Spirit" from pupil to teacher. In an un-
lucky moment he has been imprisoned by the giant Galapas,
a scoundrelly character who talks a great deal like Benito
Mussolini.[8] Fortunately, however, this medieval fascist is much
confused by the arrival of Arthur and Merlyn (who are invisible as long as they hold hands, which they cannot always
manage) and the timely intervention of Pellinore's devoted
Questing Beast, which chases the tyrant into his highest
tower. There ensues a joyous liberation of all the slaves and
captives, and Pellinore as the ranking prisoner expands with
schoolmasterly feeling:

The firelight and the cheering, with King Pellinore's encour-
aging remarks, such as "Britons never shall be slaves" or "I
hope you will never forget the lessons you have learned while
you were with us here," or "I shall always be glad to hear from
any Old Slaves, how they get on in life," . . . combined to make
the leave-taking a festive one.[9]

Imaginative scenes of this sort, and the artful flicking of the
chucklehead on the raw (without scarifying him) help to make
The Sword in the Stone one of the best books of its kind ever
written.

Yet, as I have said before, its merit does not lie in hilarious comedy alone. It is a wise book as well as a witty one, and its wisdom lies in the breadth and depth of Arthur's education. He grows well under instruction, even though he is not an exceptionally gifted boy; in fact he is a little slow — "a born follower" and hero-worshipper. His virtues, however, outweigh his defects: unswerving loyalty, physical courage, common sense, and a well-developed conscience. Life with Sir Ector was the very kind that he needed. He roamed the castle and the land near by as he pleased, absorbing without knowing it a love of animals (his dog Cavall especially) and of people. After Merlyn comes to the castle as his tutor he develops fast, and not merely in theoretical wisdom. The magician sends him and Kay on an expedition with Robin Hood and his band against the stronghold of the Anthropophagi — Scythians, Sciopods, Nisites, and other revolting creatures — who have been stalking honest men with poisoned arrows. There Wart learns something of exact discipline and the strategy of forest warfare, and how to shoot straight and strong even though a dying Sciopod will break one's collarbone in the next instant.

It is Merlyn's instruction in more theoretical fields, however, which strengthens Arthur (and the book) immeasurably. This instruction, though highly unorthodox, is exactly what a future King would need, for it dramatizes the nature of human power. Every now and then Merlyn changes Arthur into an animal — perch, hawk, snake, owl, and badger — so that he can talk with his kind and learn the ways of life. White manages these scenes with brilliant originality. They are not in any sense of the word Aesopian apologues; they are full and leisurely discussions, with moralizing subordinated to exposition. The instruction is so obliquely presented that it slides into Arthur's mind without any effort. And the circumstances are so fascinatingly new, so dramatically vivid to a boy that the lessons learned there would fasten themselves in the mind forever. A whole new world is opened up to Wart—the strange, murky depths of the castle moat, with a shoal of sticklebacks performing their precise evolutions, a swan suspended "like a Zeppelin" on the surface above; a world of lurking danger also, in the form of the great pike who rules the moat and who talks with the perch, Arthur, on the Might which is Right. Only at the last moment does the boy-fish escape those danger-ous jaws. The variety of these scenes is amazing. From the hawks Arthur learns the rigorous discipline of a military caste; with the snake, cosily lying under the grasses, he talks of animal life aeons before, and how an inoffensive reptile was slain by "H. Sapiens armatus georgius sanctus"; the owl takes him to the goddess Athene, who causes him to have a stupen-dous dream of the creation of the world, a scene of sweeping imagination ending with a glimpse of man, who fashions an arrowhead and slays his brother; the kindly, somewhat pedan-tic badger shows Arthur the virtues of tidy domesticity and reads him a parable from his treatise (being prepared for the D.Litt.) on the trustful relationship between God and Man.

The lessons learned in these transformations sink into Wart's mind and strengthen his arm at a crucial moment. For White parts from Malory in one important respect: the sword does not come out of the stone at Arthur's first pull. At that moment his friends come to his aid:

There was a kind of rushing noise, and a long chord played along with it. All round the churchyard there were hundreds of old friends. They rose over the church wall all together, like the Punch and Judy ghosts of remembered days, and there were otters and nightingales and vulgar crows and hares and serpents and falcons and fishes and goats and dogs and dainty

unicorns and newts and solitary wasps and goat-moth cater-
pillars and corkindrills and volcanoes and mighty trees and
patient stones. They loomed round the church wall, the lovers
and helpers of the Wart, and they all spoke solemnly in turn.
Some of them had come from the banners in the church,
where they were painted in heraldry, some from the waters
and the sky and the fields about, but all, down to the smallest
shrew mouse, had come to help on account of love. Wart felt
his power grow.

The friends speak to Arthur, reminding him of the lessons he
has learned. Then the miracle happens:

The Wart walked up to the great sword for the third time. He
put out his right hand softly and drew it out as gently as from
a scabbard.[10]

With this first of Arthur's great victories his carefree boyhood ends. It had been a glorious time, filled with enough
danger to test him, and enough hilarious companionship to
sweeten the somewhat solemn cast of his mind. As he approaches manhood, shades of the prison house begin to close
on him. Toward the close of the book he tells Merlyn what
he would do if he were knighted: "I should pray to God to
let me encounter all the evil in the world in my own person,
so that if I conquered there should be none left, while if I
were defeated, it would be I who would suffer for it." As
Arthur's formal education comes to an end one realizes that
the time of real testing lies ahead, and so it proves as White
carries the career of the King forward in *The Witch in the
Wood* and *The Ill-Made Knight*. Below the last line of text in
The Sword in the Stone appropriately appears the legend "The
Beginning."

The Witch in the Wood (1939) shifts the scene to another

part of Britain, the raw northern land of Lothian and Orkney. Far to the south Arthur hovers over the story, but the attention is fixed on his half sister and her family. Morgause, the wife of King Lot, is a very strange person indeed. Her people think of her as a witch, and small wonder, for while she apparently is not up to performing transformations and the other elementary tricks of sorceresses, she keeps everyone in a stew by her fantastic behavior. White uses the broadest strokes of burlesque in showing a woman of kaleidoscopic whims and passing fancies. She has a strong if misdirected dramatic sense; to beguile an ill-fated fisherboy, for example, she plays a bewildering succession of roles, among them The Lonely Spirit, Voyaging through Strange Seas of Thought Alone; The Venus of Milo; Mother Love; The Spirit of Empire; and Miss Lothian and Orkney — 1470! Life in her household is rather disorganized; her husband Lot is away during most of the story, fighting against Arthur, and her sons Gawaine, Gareth, Gaheris, and Agravaine are left to the instruction of a bewildered Saracen tutor, Palomides. Her court is visited by two friends we have already met in *The Sword in the Stone*, King Pellinore and Sir Grummore Grummursum, who add comic confusion to the writing of poetry, a tournament on ice, and the hunt of the Questing Beast. The story ends — or better, the series of episodes breaks off — when Arthur defeats Lot and the other rebellious kings at the Battle of Bedegraine. In a flurry of new loyalty and social excitement all hands go to Arthur's court for Pellinore's wedding to his "Piggy," the Queen's daughter of Flanders, where, by Morgause's wiles Mordred is conceived.

Readers who were swept away by *The Sword in the Stone* were somewhat puzzled by White's second venture. It is not up to its predecessor by a long shot. In the first place, the general situation is not nearly so interesting. A great deal of the strength in *The Sword* sprang from Arthur's careful preparation for the kingship which is the very focus of the whole cycle. Under Merlyn's wise if unorthodox instruction Wart grows before our eyes; the story develops to a high end. In *The Witch* the development of Britain under the King's rule is subordinated to the miscellaneous antics of a group of comic eccentrics. Secondly, as a consequence, the humor of *The Witch* often seems adventitious rather than integral; it is less spontaneous, less the result of important events in the story and more apt to rely on slapstick and farce. Finally, *The Witch* lacks the imaginative invention which made *The Sword* not only superlative comedy but something more. There is nothing in the later novel, for example, to match the scenes in which Merlyn transforms his pupil into various animals and reveals to him the nature of the world. In these scenes White gives a depth and breadth to his story which he was not able to repeat in dealing with Lothian.

Even so, the comedy in *The Witch in the Wood* is often hilarious. Though Morgause is usually fantastic rather than funny, once in a while she is quite amusing. White lets himself go in describing the elaborate "magic" ritual by which she preserves her beauty (a ritual based on advices from the magazine *Vague*). Her bath is a gruesome mess compounded of equal parts of goat's milk, pig's blood, sea water, mud, and white of egg! Pellinore and Grummore also are up to their old waggish ways. There is good fun in the account of the Questing Beast. To console the lovelorn Pellinore, Grummore and Palomides make an elaborate representation of the animal he had hunted so long. The situation becomes involved when the real Beast appears and falls in love with her counterfeit, animated by Grummore at the front end and Palomides at the rear. An awkward period ensues, in which the Beast besieges

Lothian Castle hopefully. Finally Merlyn suggests that the only remedy is psychoanalysis. This clears up the wretched animal's fixation, though the cure involves the transfer of her affection to the analyst, Palomides. When last we see the Beast she is trotting along behind the northern party bound for Pellinore's wedding, keeping a wary eye on the Saracen.

It is not hard to understand her affection for Palomides, for he is an amazing character. In reviving Malory's muddled and mercurial paynim, White shows the originality and imaginative daring in adapting old material that have marked the outstanding re-creations of the legend, especially in our own day. Palomides is more than funny, he is whimsical, a little pathetic, and very likable:

He was a very learned man, who had been educated in one of the bardic schools of the East, with a large, round shiny face and horn-rimmed spectacles. The whites of his eyes were shot with a sort of toffee color. He was charming, but not good at teaching boys.[11]

His language is a mixture of misapplied slang, quaint twists of idiom and syntax, and learned tags. On one occasion he ventures to help Pellinore in a sonnet he is composing to his love, "Piggy." The King's complete ignorance of prosody ("'Yours truly observes no rhymes, respected royalty,' said Sir Palomides") finally drives the paynim wild!

Sir Palomides started to scream at the top of his voice. It was suddenly too much for him.

"Not done! Not done!" he began shouting, tearing King Pellinore's poem into fragments and stamping upon them. "Dense! Dense! This is crass! Oh, my! Not done! God Almighty, help poor babus (D. V.)! Nothing is understood by anybody ever. Immortal swan of Thames i.e. Chaucer, what sins are committed in thy name? Poesy, first born progeny of honored Muses! Death and damnation (figuratively speaking). My head, my head! Beg pardon all. Excuse precipitate exit. Ta-Ta!"

And with these confused remarks Sir Palomides rushed out of the room, clutching his temples with both hands.[12]

His distress is understandable when we learn that he is a poet himself. In fact we are allowed to see one of the sonnets from a cycle he composed in honor of La Beale Isoud — a remarkable piece, scrupulous in meter and rhyme:

> *Hon. Madam! Kind regards! Immortal life*
> *Be yours henceforth from 18th ultimo,*
> *Is prayer which Palomides sings to fife*
> *And tabor twice per diem. May you know*
> *Ten thousand offspring (male) legitimate,*
> *Each one well blessed with twenty thousand wives!*
> *May each and all achieve whate'er he strives*
> *With L. S. D., (D. V.), and godly fate.*
> *May God Almighty, whom you much resemble*
> *Send cows and elephants to crowd your bed*
> *Waving their lofty trunks which squirm and tremble*
> *To shade from sol your most respected head.*
> *Kind Madam, Grand-Pa of this humble fish,*
> *Calicut (failed) B. A., accept this wish.*[13]

Next to Palomides, King Lot is the most amusing person in the book, even though he appears seldom. White again shows his wit in combining the ancient and the modern, for in many ways Lot is the choleric colonel of British cartoons, the chuckleheaded, testy professional soldier. His letter to Morgause describing the battle of Bedegraine is a masterpiece. It is not only good narrative (White follows Malory's account in Book I of the *Morte Darthur* closely) but excellent satire. The battle was very disturbing to Lot's British sense of the fitness of things:

The whole war has been an absolute surprise for everybody, and everything has been done in a most unusual way, not at all what one is accustomed to, and *not* what we should have called sporting when I was a boy. None of these people understood the science of war. I told the Kings repeatedly what to expect, but nobody would pay me any attention, and now we have lost it. The discipline was not British. You can't do anything without discipline.

Lot's letter is a catalogue of complaints, ranging from peevish comment on the fact that his "woolies" had never arrived, to Arthur's duplicity in making an "anti-aggression pact" with King Bors of France. Merlyn comes in for hard treatment, not only because he advised Arthur to make the alliance with Bors but also because he suggested a surprise attack at night, catching Lot's host in their collapsed pavilions. And the state of morale is a matter for deep concern:

[The army] seemed to be absolutely without patriotism. No spirit. The New Army all over.... I hear that our casualties were forty-six thousand. I put it down to unfair use of magicians.

Yet with a beautifully inconsistent and characteristic about-face Lot ends on a note of national pride:

I am bringing back an Unknown Warrior to bury at Lothian. Our men were magnificent.[14]

The national picture, though definitely submerged by comedy, is not entirely forgotten in *The Witch in the Wood*. We see Arthur briefly, and we hear him getting straight talk from

Merlyn on the dangerous possibilities in his new kingdom, where Might still seems to be Right:

Look at England [Merlyn says]: look at all the barns burnt, and dead men's legs sticking out of ponds, and horses with swelled bellies by the roadside, and mills falling down, and money buried, and nobody daring to walk abroad with gold or ornaments on their clothes. That's chivalry nowadays.[15]

Arthur takes Merlyn's words to heart, for he was a teachable young man, and he sets about establishing a new kind of knighthood "to bind Might" and suppress the anarchy of private will. The Round Table was to be a means of breeding a "new generation of chivalry." And the battle of Bedegraine, by which Arthur overthrew the confederation of disaffected and violent Kings, was the first step in the master design which we see even more clearly in *The Ill-Made Knight. The Witch in the Wood* therefore has a legitimate place in the grand cycle of Arthur's rise and fall which White is still in process of completing.

It resembles his other books also in its vivid presentation of medieval scene. As in *The Sword in the Stone*, White translates a scholarly knowledge of Malory's England into swift modern prose. He seems thoroughly at home in castles, and describes the stronghold at Lothian as though he had lived there all his life. And he takes us bodily to Arthur's great camp on the eve of Bedegraine: the forest of brightly colored pavilions, enormous knights beside them playing chess, cooks plagued by thieving dogs, and a motley crowd of vivandières, gipsies, joculators, troubadours, bear-dancers, and mountebanks. He also introduces curious bits of medieval lore. For example, Palomides shows Grummore a great vellum manuscript illustrated with pictures of the fabulous animals dear to medievalists — Griffins, Bonnacons, Manticores, Dragons, and the like — as a prelude to the beautiful yet brutal scene in which the four sons of Morgause slay a white, daintily stepping unicorn.[16]

As we take leave of T. H. White we are struck by the fact that he has written Arthurian comedy of a very high order without losing sight of the heroic legend. Even in his first two books, where his intention is generally comic, he gives us a sense of the tragic story unfolding. In *The Ill-Made Knight*, apart from a few humorous interludes such as the discovery of Elaine in the boiling bath and the abduction of Guenever by the cockney knight, Sir Meliagrance, the tone is generally serious and even tense. This reconciliation of the two worlds of humorous and heroic experience is accomplished with freshness and originality by a mind teeming with the pageantry of Arthur's career. Sir Dagonet — and Sir Launcelot too — would have found T. H. White a rare companion.

The Seer of Caledon and Camelot

Merlin has taken on new importance in the twentieth century. Modern writers have daringly reworked old material, in some cases giving the seer more human depth and mystical power than he ever had before. In other chapters, I discuss the Merlin of E. A. Robinson, T. H. White, and Charles Williams, particularly as he plays his part in the "Tragedy of Camelot." Here I shall describe additional works in which he is important, especially as the agent of vast supernatural powers. This last is given added force by renewed interest in the Caledonian Merlin, Merlinus Silvestris, the tortured sage of the *Vita Merlini,* attributed to Geoffrey of Monmouth.

The thorny matter of the connection between Merlin of Caledon and the seer of Camelot will probably never be resolved, and I shall certainly not try to do so here. It is enough to say that leading authorities believe them to have been one and the same.[1] However that may be, the connection of Merlinus Silvestris with Arthur, tenuous at best, was severed shortly after Geoffrey wrote and has largely remained so among modern authors. In fact, the story virtually disappeared after the Middle Ages, and has been revived only recently.

As found in the *Vita Merlini*, Merlin is a king and prophet who helps Rodarchus of Cumberland and Peredur of North Wales in war against the King of Scotland. The Scots are overcome, but Merlin is so shaken by the loss of his three brothers in battle that he flees to the Caledonian forest, distracted. There he lives the rest of his life, giving vent to his woe and exercising strange prophetic powers. Several times he returns to the court, for his sister Ganieda, his wife Gwendoloena, and King Rodarchus still cherish hopes of saving him. But soon he goes back to his forest. Of the other crowded and disjointed episodes in the story there is no need to write, save to mention that Merlin informs Rodarchus that his wife has been unfaithful to him and, finally, that on one occasion Taliesin joins Merlin in the forest and gives him a long account of Avalon, where he has taken Arthur after his battle with Mordred. Geoffrey's poem ends with Merlin still alive; in other versions of the tale he meets a violent death.

The resuscitation of Merlinus Silvestris in the last twenty years was anticipated in John Veitch's *Merlin,* published (with other poems) at Edinburgh in 1889. In his preliminary remarks Veitch is careful to explain that the hero of his poem is Merlinus Caledonius and not the seer of Camelot. He then outlines the Caledonian legend (roughly paralleling the account in the *Vita Merlini*) and closes with remarks on Merlin's religious belief, which seems to have fused certain Christian ideas (though he never embraced Christianity) and nature worship. The poem itself is largely a lament by Merlin in his forest refuge. His sister Gwendydd and the spirit of his first love, Hwimileian, do their best to comfort him. Finally he is

captured by a group of furious herdsmen and drowned in the
river Tweed, without, I might add, much agitation on the part
of the reader. Veitch was no more of a poet than was necessary
to produce what is sometimes known as respectable verse. Yet
his literary gifts are of much less consequence than the fact
that the Caledonian Merlin had emerged from his dark forest,
and that he carried with him the promise of spiritual rather
than merely magical powers.

The seer of Caledon is united with his alter ego of Arthur's
court in Gordon Bottomley's dramatic sketch, "Merlin's Grave"
(published in *Scenes and Plays,* 1929). The scene is laid near
a lake in present-day Scotland. On an island there lives a lady
who, ages past, had known Merlin and laid him under enchantment. He refers to her as the Lady of the Lake, and
reminds her of the day when Pellinore brought her to Arthur's
court. In essence, it is the story of the imprisonment of Merlin
by Nimue, but here it concerns the northern seer. A shadowy
presence within a thorn tree, Merlin pleads with the Lady
for love and release:

> *You would not come again,*
> *Did you not mean to be dear*
> *And end the pain.*
> *Let me out: give to me, give*
> *That virgin loveliness*
> *That ages have made not less*
> *And your deeds cannot impair:*
> *Come to me, let me live.*
> *Reverence and fear surround me,*
> *Might has wearied me,*
> *In those isolations love had not found me,*
> *Women had let me be:*
> *Yet I cannot grow old in my heart*
> *Or keep from desiring loveliness.*[2]

134

The Lady in turn extracts a secret of Merlin's magic so as to make him invisible. On his instructions she winds thread from a spindle round and round the thorn and the sage disappears. Then she comes out of a trancelike state to the reproaches of a woman who has observed the imprisonment, terribly moved and frightened by what she has done.

Unlike Veitch's *Merlin,* Bottomley's poem has literary merit. It suggests the depths of mysteries remote from human experience, besides describing a Merlin who loves and suffers as men have always done. Finally, it is interesting to note that like Arthur Machen, J. C. Powys, Charles Williams, and C. S. Lewis, Bottomley conceives of an Arthurian episode as a timeless experience, as valid today as in the remote past. The "Curtain-Bearer," who acts as one of the Chorus, strikes this note of indivisible continuity at the very end:

> *Who can know*
> *What things the ancients have laid on us?*
> *A secret thing that one of us does*
> *Can be remembered and done again*
> *By flesh that is not yet born of our pain.*[3]

It is quite possible that Bottomley's attention was directed to Merlin by his friend Laurence Binyon. For in his Introduction to Binyon's posthumous *The Madness of Merlin* (1947) Bottomley speaks of Binyon's interest in the Merlin theme shortly after the performance of his play *Arthur* at the "Old Vic" in 1923, six years before the publication of "Merlin's Grave." This long-standing interest bore good fruit; *The Madness of Merlin* deserves an honored place among modern Arthurian pieces.

In Binyon's poetic drama it is again the Caledonian Merlin who is the center of the story. Bottomley explains in the introduction that the poem is based on Geoffrey's *Vita Merlini,* with some additional help from Welsh sources. The story takes place after the battle of Arthuret, in which Merlin and Redderech of North Wales defeat the heathen Scots. Driven out of his wits by memories of the three strong and beautiful sons of Mor whom he had slain, Merlin flees to the forest and there lives in a world half illusion and half mystical vision. He is visited by his sister Gwyndyth, but his wife Gwendolen, wrongly thinking him a coward for leaving the battle, renounces him. Although he returns to the court twice — on the second occasion opening Redderech's eyes to the adultery of his queen, Langoreth — the world of men cannot hold him, and he returns to the wild wood. The poem ends with the maiden Himilian bringing him comfort after dark and terrible dreams. At the very close she prophesies that a child will be born to them.

As it stands, *The Madness of Merlin* is a fragment, the first of three projected parts. The plan for the remainder of the poem, however, is explained in a letter Binyon wrote January 27, 1942:

The theme [of Part II] is Merlin's discovery (after his failure to make himself invulnerable and independent of every one in Part I) that he needs the experience of love and suffering to be complete; and this might be brought home to him through the son whom Himilian (=Nimüe or Vivien) is to bear him. I want to illustrate the way things always turn out differently from what one expects, and the results of excessive idealism (Rhydderech).... Part III is planned to be mostly dialogue about Utopias (the search for happiness) — Atlantis, the Fortunate Isles, etc.[4]

The Merlin of Binyon's poem is far from the usual enchanter and court counselor. He seems to be part (yet an uncomprehending part) of the vastness and the terror of the universe. He was not made for the world, nor the world for him. His sister Gwyndyth remembers him in his boyhood:

> *I remember how, but a boy,*
> *Suddenly he would seem a stranger among us.*
> *As if he had wandered out in a strange land*
> *Seeing us no more; and then as suddenly*
> *His spirit would return to the use of the body;*
> *But to none told he ever in what land he had been.*
> *Now, as I guess,*
> *It was some blinding vision from above*
> *Estranged the world to him.*[5]

Completely unlike the Merlin of Charles Williams' Arthurian poems (described in Chapter VII), he recoils in horror before his supernatural insight. King Redderech says to him:

> *Surely I think that by some special grace*
> *Thou mayest have pierced beyond*
> *The ranging of our eyes, and the gross sense*
> *We others use,*
> *To pluck a flower of light in a strange world.*

Merlin replies:

> *I dreamed that I was free,*
> *But such freedom is not for mortal mind.*
> *I am affrighted by my own vision.*[6]

Whereas the visions of Williams' Merlin are revelations of the lucent and almost geometrical Divine Order shaping the life of the spirit, the dreams of Binyon's Merlin — if indeed they can be called dreams and not hallucinations — are glimpses into a world of disordered terror. Such a visitation comes to him immediately after the battle:

I saw
Arising swift out of the shadowy earth
Inconceivably spreading, silently rushing
Upward and upward, covering the sky,
A vine, a fruitful vine, all bloom and abundance,
Heavy with happy clusters, with a myriad leaves.
And there were stars in heaven: it overspread the stars,
They shone between the branches and the curled tendrils.
The world was roofed with stars and with the vine's glory.
And then an arm, a naked arm, I saw,
A hand rising, and in the hand a sword
Flashing; it struck among the ripe clusters
And furiously it lopt and tore the spirting grapes.
Like thunder — rain drops fell,
Like blood; it was the blood of joy
Man's joy, the blood of men,
And in the darkness men were drunken with that blood.[7]

The overwhelming despair that surges through a highly sensitive man attuned to extraworldly impression gives Binyon's poem unusual force. Yet it is the force of pathos rather than tragedy, for Merlin seems almost entirely bounded by his own suffering. He is Job, without the Voice out of the Whirlwind. The Christianity which the saintly Kentigern tries to bring to his aid is of little avail, for (and here Binyon is poles apart from Williams) the Christian God and mystical apperception cannot fuse in Merlin. The union was there for the making, and even in terms which suggest Williams' concept of the divinely ordained "Empire" — the Romano-Byzantine imperium — which, as Williams explains, it is Merlin's and Taliessin's purpose to establish in Britain. Kentigern speaks nobly of Rome as the center of Christendom:

> *Shall we not then rejoice*
> *That at this edge and outpost of the world*

We are chosen to be imperilled, to uphold
The heavenly Kingdom that remembers us
Even among the mountains and the mists
Accompanying us with shining of the swords
Of angels; martyrs in the glory of their wounds;
Myriads of spirits, with heart-storming sound
Of blown trumpets and the on-rushing of wings
Above, around, beside us, in the day and in the night-time,
One infinite society of earth and heaven.[8]

Yet the fusion into "one infinite society" never occurs in Binyon's poem. Merlin cannot escape his private furies, and Kentigern, when the chance for illuminated understanding occurs, sees the sufferer only as willfully intransigent.

Even admitting the somewhat inconclusive development of Binyon's poem, however (and remembering that he might have broadened the scope in the parts never completed), *The Madness of Merlin* is an impressive work. Apart from its majestic picture of suffering, it is probably fair to say that under happier conditions Binyon's Merlin might have found himself at home in Williams' region of the summer stars.

A more recent work, while it does not have the tumultuous and frustrated passion of *The Madness of Merlin*, shows Merlin as a preserver and prophet of Christianity in Britain. In 1948 Christopher Fry, a dramatist who has shown unusual strength especially in *The Lady's Not for Burning* and *A Sleep of Prisoners*, wrote *Thor, With Angels* for production at the Canterbury Festival. The story takes place at the time of St. Augustine's evangelizing visitation to Britain in the year 596. Cymen, a Jute who has settled in England, returns to his farm after a campaign, having horrified his sons by unaccountably sparing the life of Hoel, a young Briton, whom he brings back a captive. From Cymen's explanation it is evident that his hand was stayed by a supernatural power, and as the play develops it is clear that this power is God; for while Hoel is not consciously a believer, he inherits remnants and memories of primitive British Christianity. The upshot of the play is that Cymen, against the strong opposition of his family, goes to welcome St. Augustine.

During the course of tense conflict over the fate of Hoel — Cymen's sons wishing to sacrifice him to the pagan gods — Merlin appears, having been found in a caved-in quarry, bearing with him two sorrows: the love of a woman once his own, for whom he walks the earth besotted, and the loss of his zeal after the death of Arthur. It is his function in the play not so much to save Hoel and turn Cymen to Christianity as to provide the prophetic insight and the confidence in God's slow but inevitable processes of salvation which make any other ending out of the question. He speaks almost as a detached, omniscient Greek chorus, predicting assimilation of the Germanic invaders by the British, telling of the Christian land of Arthur, of Joseph of Arimathea's flowering thorn, and of the persistent dreams: the gradual re-forming of old shapes and beliefs and gods into the pattern of God's will.

Apart from Cymen's conflict both internal and external, *Thor, With Angels* is a contemplative play of devoutness and dignity. And it is Merlin who gives it this quality. He is not only the familiar figure of legend, the offspring of a dark and mysterious birth, Arthur's trusted counselor, and the victim of a predatory woman; he is also the seer who has experienced terrible defeat yet who is the harbinger of God's new kingdom in Britain. Like his counterpart in the poems of Charles Williams, Christopher Fry's Merlin is one of the shapers and movers of belief.

In the remainder of this chapter I shall outline briefly the part Merlin has played recently as a central figure in the story of the Grail. Though a more detailed discussion is to be found in the next chapter the following remarks may help to emphasize his functional importance as an agent of Light.

In *A Glastonbury Romance* (1933) John Cowper Powys associates Merlin with the Grail. John Geard, mayor of the modern city of Glastonbury, in his attempt to revive the ancient spiritual meaning of the place, seems to think of himself as a new Merlin. Several other allusions in the book make it clear that Powys conceives of the Welsh seer as the active, unseen force in Glastonbury, which (of all the "reservoirs of world-magic") has "the largest residue of unused power." It is clear, however, that Powys' Grail is a far different vessel from the Sacred Cup of Charles Williams; in fact it seems as much the Celtic cauldron of Ceridwen as a Christian chalice.

Williams spectacularly restores the Grail to the important place it held in the romances of the Middle Ages, and with this restoration raises Merlin to a position of the highest importance. With brilliant imagination he unites the old legend of Merlin's parentage — the union of a demon and a mortal maiden — with an explanation of the seer's mystical function. A passage in his novel *Descent into Hell* (1937) puts the matter clearly:

It is said in the old tales that the devil longs to become incarnate that he may challenge the Divine Word in his own chosen house of flesh and that he therefore once desired and overshadowed a maid. But even at the moment of conception a mystical baptism fell on the child, and the devil was cast out of his progeny at the moment of entrance. He who was born of that purified intercourse with angelic sacrilege was Merlin, who, wisest of magicians, prophesied and prefigured the Grail-quest, and built a chapel to serve the Table till Logres came to an end, and the Merciful Child Galahad discovered the union in a Mass of the Holy Ghost which was sung by Messias among a great company of angels.[9]

This concept of Merlin is central to the meaning of Williams' Arthurian poems, especially *Taliessin Through Logres* (1938) and *The Region of the Summer Stars* (1944), in which the seer's traditional function as the agent of Arthur's coming to power is absorbed in his greater responsibility to establish the holy kingdom of Logres in Britain. In this role he is Time, or Timelessness personified; his very nature makes him a part of the illimitable powers of Light above and about the earth. That his holy kingdom finally collapses in the red disaster at Camlan is not a fatal defeat, for the hero in whose birth he was so largely instrumental achieves the Grail. And though the Sacred Vessel is withdrawn for a time, it is not lost forever.

Merlin also plays an important part in C. S. Lewis' novel *That Hideous Strength* (1946). Though the Grail itself does not figure in the story, the powers implicit in it are the final means of overthrowing a diabolical conspiracy to seize control of modern England and indeed to create a new kind of man which is a monstrous perversion of the old. Merlinus Ambrosius, resuscitated after long centuries of sleep under Bragdon Wood, joins the little "Company" headed by Mr. Fisher-King which finally saves England from disaster. Lewis makes him a vivid and lifelike figure, almost a giant of a man, with reddish-grey hair and beard. He talks to Mr. Fisher-King in grave Latin sentences, shot through occasionally with flashes of the wild Celt he is in no small measure. We learn a good deal about him in Dr. Dimble's conversation with Jane Studdock:

Has it ever struck you what an odd creation Merlin is? He's not evil; yet he's a magician. He is obviously a druid; yet he knows all about the Grail. He's "the devil's son"; but then Layamon goes out of his way to tell you that the kind of being who fathered Merlin needn't have been bad after all. You remember, "There dwell in the sky many kinds of wights. Some of them are good, and some work evil." . . . I often wonder . . . whether Merlin doesn't represent the last trace of something the later tradition has quite forgotten about — something that became impossible when the only people in touch with the supernatural were either white or black, either priests or sorcerers.[10]

To be sure, Merlin's ancient "Atlantean" power is insufficient in itself, and even unlawful, as Mr. Fisher-King explains; yet when combined with the transplanetary forces of Divine Grace flowing through the "Company" it is vitally important in bringing about the downfall of the satanic conspiracy. Thus, though Merlin is an ally rather than the prime mover, as in Williams' poems, he occupies a very strong strategic position.

Merlin has come a long way from Nennius' supernatural boy who prophesied to King Vortigern, from Geoffrey's combination of Welsh bard and prophet, and indeed even from the magician and seer of Malory. But his development in modern times has been governed by the logic of the past. As we see him today in Charles Williams and C. S. Lewis, he is the inevitable product of the beneficent supernatural powers which had always set him apart from other men.

SEVEN

The Spiritual Land of Logres

In the Foreword to *Arthur Pendragon of Britain*, an adaptation of Malory's *Morte Darthur* published in New York in 1943, the editor, John W. Donaldson, makes a remarkable statement. He says that he has omitted entirely from his edition such allegorical material as the Quest for the Holy Grail, and as much as he could of the story of Joseph of Arimathea. He continues:

These episodes, which must have had their source in monkish interpolation in earlier folk-lore, introduce monastic ideas of sin, chastity and penance entirely foreign to all other parts of the tale.... Unfortunately, this religious or spiritual quality has ... colored popular revisions ... of Malory. This, I feel, has given rise to a generally false impression of the tale and of the character of Arthur and his knights.

In thus excising the Holy Grail even more completely than Robinson or Erskine had ever done, Donaldson unconsciously expressed a point of view which had already been rejected in some of the most significant and original work ever done in the Arthurian story. The most exciting development of the legend in our day has been the re-establishment of the Grail by Charles Williams and others as a profound spiritual force. Williams particularly rejected the various degrees and shades of disbelief which color a great deal of Arthurian writing. In him and others like him, the Grail is restored to the mystical place it held in certain of the medieval romances, and the "Tragedy of Camelot" is played within the vast framework of the struggle between the Powers of Light and Darkness. The title of his Arthurian novel, *War in Heaven*, is completely appropriate.

Williams ran counter to powerful forces in restoring the Grail to its old position. The skeptical temper of a world shaken as never before in history stood squarely in his way. Under the blows of war and economic disaster, a monstrous evil had beset Christianity; at its most melodramatic, a heaping up by tens of thousands of the innocent slain in ghetto and concentration camp; at its least, a calculated rejection of "uncertain" spiritual benefits in favor of material security. Williams also disagreed with those scholars who believe that the Grail legend, as it emerged in the Middle Ages, is pagan rather than Christian in origin. This school holds that the Grail was a miraculous vessel of the Celts, piously and inventively transferred to Christian stories, and its rites are shown to have resemblances with primitive ceremonies.[1] Ever since 1888, when Alfred Nutt published his *Studies on the Legend of the Holy Grail*, scholars have been much influenced by the theory that the Grail originated in ancient Celtic or other pagan legend. Miss Jessie L. Weston, in *From Ritual to Romance* (1920), associated the story with primitive fertility rites, as in the ceremonies of the Adonis cult.[2] R. S. Loomis and A. C. L. Brown have made striking contributions respectively in *Celtic Myth and Arthurian Romance* (1927)[3] and *The Origin of the*

Grail Legend (1943). Despite the weight of recent authority, however, Williams has rejected the pagan origin of the legend, and in doing so has created works of high originality and literary power.

Strange as it may seem in so confirmed a Celticist, John Cowper Powys has some importance in giving spiritual elevation to the Grail. Though he stressed pagan myth and feeling far more than Christian, he often associated the Grail with the ineffable mysteries of religious or quasi-religious belief.

Celtic legends play a very important part in two of Powys' novels. As a boy at Sherborne School near Cadbury he remembered hearing local antiquarians say that Arthur and his knights played at chess within Cadbury Hill.[4] And in his essay "My Welsh Home" (in *Obstinate Cymric*, 1947), he speaks of his feeling at Corwen that he was living in the story of "Kilwch and Olwen," amid creatures immemorially old. His Welsh inheritance is poured out lavishly in *A Glastonbury Romance* (1933) and *Maiden Castle* (1936).

The first of these, a sprawling story of eleven hundred and seventy-four pages, concerns the attempt made by John Geard, Mayor of Glastonbury, to restore the modern town to the great place it once held as a center of faith. Despite his confidence in mysterious powers which he seems to feel link him with Merlin, he is not entirely successful. He is bitterly opposed by Philip Crow and others who represent the "forces of reason," and who wish industrial rather than spiritual development for the town. A great pageant presenting religious and mythical scenes has to be halted in performance when the antiquary, Owen Evans, suspended on the cross as Christ, so associates himself with the Saviour that he breaks a blood vessel. Even miracles performed by Geard at the "Grail Fountain" on Chalice Hill do not win him victory. A flood from the sea inundates the region, and does much damage to Glastonbury itself. In attempting to rescue his enemy Philip Crow, Geard is drowned, perhaps by suicide. This is the gist of the situation, so far as it concerns this study. It would be impossible to give in a few words any adequate picture of this highly populated, tangled, and emotionally mystical book.

The interest for us at the moment lies in the way Powys deals with the legend of the Grail. In *A Glastonbury Romance,* the Grail is a pagan, Celtic concept, thinly overlaid with Christian belief. While John Geard is outwardly a Christian, and while the second section of his great pageant portrays the Passion of Christ, actually he represents immemorially primitive forces. There is no reason to doubt Owen Evans in his belief that Geard was linked with "the old magical powers." The Grail itself, so far as it is seen in the novel, is not truly Christian, even in Sam Dekker's vision of it as a crystal chalice with two handles, filled with dark water, streaked with blood, in which a fish swam. It is usually assumed to be an ancient Celtic vessel. Evans, for example, longs to pierce the mystery of "the Cauldron of Yr Echwyd . . . the undying grail,"[5] and he speaks fervently to Lady Rachel Zoyland and Ned Athling about the ancient Cymric traditions of Glastonbury:

Few Glastonbury people realise that they are actually living in *yr Echwyd,* the land of Annwn, the land of twilight and death, where the shores are of Mortuorum Mare, the Sea of the Departed. This place has always been set apart . . . from the earliest times . . . Urien the Mysterious, Avallach the Unknown, were Fisher Kings here . . . and for what did they fish? The Triads only dare to hint at these things. . . .

. . . . . .

They sought for more than a fish, . . . they sought for the knot of the opposites, for the clasping of the Two Twilights, for the mingling place of the waters, for the fusion of the metals, for the bride-bed of the contradictions, for the copulation-cry of the Yes and No, for the amalgam of the Is and Is Not!...what the Fisher Kings of my people sought, and no other priests of no other race on earth have ever sought it ...was not only the Cauldron and the Spear...not only the Mwys of Gwyddno and the Sword of Arthur, but that which exists in the moment of timeless time when these two are one!...

What they sought was Parthenogenesis and the Self-Birth of Psyche.[6]

What interests us at the moment is not the murky, mystical paradoxes of Powys in this passage but rather his strange pagan exaltation. This paganism is responsible, among other things, for connecting the Grail somehow with erotic experience. The long, confused scene at Mother Legge's bawdyhouse is a case in point. Powys seems here to be suggesting a kind of religious prostitution within the framework of the Grail story. Mother Legge's house, according to one of the inmates, was known as "Camelot," and at the end of the scene John Geard seizes on a big silver bowl, apparently symbolizing the Grail, in a kind of religious ecstasy. Powys is even more specific in another passage:

The presence of the Grail in that spot has the effect of digging deep channels for the amorous life of those who touch its soil. ...None approach these three Glastonbury hills without an intensification of whatever erotic excitement they are capable of.[7]

Powys and Charles Williams, therefore, are poles apart in their concept of the Holy Vessel. Yet in a curious sense they touch. Both of them conceive the Grail as a force so titanic that it almost eludes comprehension. Powys speaks of this force as "the knot of the opposites . . . the amalgam of the Is and Is Not." Though he is much less rewarding when we get to the root of his paradoxes (if indeed we can) than Williams, there is in both men the unmistakable feeling that in the presence of the greatest mysteries we must often seem to speak in riddles. Even more specific a resemblance to Williams is found in Powys' assumption that Geard's controversy with the "forces of reason" in Glastonbury is something like a grand warfare between good and evil. This is not, of course, Williams' Christian conflict, yet it is hard to believe that Powys had not read *War in Heaven* when he wrote of the great wave of antipathy which centered all the hatreds for the Grail in the sleeping mind of John Crow. Here for the moment forces are built up to "kill" the Grail by a kind of psychic annihilation. One remembers the remarkable scene in *War in Heaven* describing Gregory Persimmons' attempt to destroy the Sacred Vessel at a distance by diabolical means, and while Williams does far better than Powys, there is no overlooking the fact that Powys has also taken the Grail into a vast, supernatural realm.

Powys' *Maiden Castle*, though not nearly so full and vivid in its use of Arthurian myth as *A Glastonbury Romance*, shows the same attitude toward primitive material. Here Celtic mysticism is caught up in the person of the striking, grotesque Enoch Quirm, who lives near ancient Mai-Dun Castle. Like Geard in the earlier novel, Quirm seems to be the reincarnation of a legendary hero, in this case Urien. Yet he also appears to be a kind of transmigratory holding company, representing King Pellam, Uther, and Bran the Blessed! — a band of worthies who seem to give him uneasy company. He has the mythical insight of an early Welsh seer and has deeply studied Cymric tradition:

I had always guessed that what the ancients called "the mysteries" had their parallel in Welsh tradition, but it wasn't till I learnt to read the *old* Welsh books that I came on the track of a whole cycle of ancient gods, connected in one way or another with "the mysteries", that's to say with the worship of the great goddess Carridwen.[8]

On the basis of these studies he wishes to "break the bonds of life's natural law" and penetrate to the region where love and hate are one. Again the paradox appears, as in Quirm's belief that the gods of Mai-Dun (of whom he is one) operate both to create and destroy. Quirm also expresses the surge of mystical feeling which lies at the heart of Powys' primitivism and which appears in its own way in Williams' Christian poems. The spring of all vital action seems to be that "old magic of the mind, [which] when driven to bay by the dogs of reality, ... turns upon the mathematical law of life and tears it to bits."[9]

In Powys, therefore, we see the Grail, even though it is largely pagan, in terms of tremendous mystical power. With Arthur Machen and especially Charles Williams this power was to be concentrated in Christian belief; Celtic primitivism was no longer the predominant force.

We have already seen something of Machen's work on the Grail. His "Great Return"[10] was a landmark in the restoration of the Holy Vessel to its ancient eucharistic significance. In a number of ways he surveyed the road which Charles Williams was to build after him. Machen insists, for example, upon the power of incantation. His essay "Celtic Magic"[11] makes the point clearly. Speaking of the Celtic genius and its function in life, he says "The only refuge for us is in incantation, in high magic; happy are they that can find the secret of this concealed mystery." This incantation, when it touches the

Holy Grail, will transmit something of the mystery caught up in the Communion of Christ with his followers, and will help illuminate a secret of surpassing importance closely held through the centuries by certain elect of the Christian faith. A passage in Machen's essay "The Holy Grail" explains this last point:

The minstrels and the monks had heard faint and distant rumour proceeding from the "Secret School" which had always been latent in the Christian Church, and, without understanding very well the real intent of the message, they constructed this marvellous story of a chalice holier than the chalice of the mass, of a Communion more intimate than that of any earthly altar, of a mass with words more mighty in their operations than the Words of Institution, of a priesthood and episcopate which held their Orders directly from God.[12]

To understand the full implications of the "Secret School" as it touches the Grail legend, let us look at a book which appears to have influened Machen strongly. In his essay "The Holy Grail" he gives high praise to A. E. Waite's *Hidden Church of the Holy Graal: Its Legends and Symbolism*.[13] Though this book has been severely attacked by Arthurian scholars — J. D. Bruce in the Bibliography of his *Evolution of Arthurian Romance* calls it "fantastic" — it deserves to be discussed in any treatment of the Grail legend in the twentieth century, for it argues the connection of the legend with Christian sacramental rather than pagan tradition.

Waite finds the heart of the Grail mystery in the passage in Robert de Borron's *Joseph of Arimathea* describing the transmission of certain secret words by Christ to St. Joseph.[14] According to Waite's interpretation, these words, which referred to the Holy Sacrament and more specifically to the Epiclesis of the Greek rite — a petition for the visitation of the

Holy Spirit to the worshippers — remained in reserve in the hands of a priesthood consecrated by Christ, and were transmitted from Keeper to Keeper in a secret way. Thus the Precious Words came down through the centuries within the consecrated fellowship of a small, highly selected, and unformalized group, within the Church and yet above it:

The Secret School towards which I look [says Waite] and of which I recognize the existence did not differ, ... in respect of Doctrine from the eternal ways of salvation, but it opened out an infinite realm which lies behind the manifest life of teaching — that realm which was in the mind of St. Augustine when he said, ... that the definition of Three Persons subsisting in one God was not an expression which satisfied the intellect, but that some kind of formulation is necessary.[15]

Waite insists on the Christian origin and nature of the legend. The Grail myth, he says, sprang from Christ's Eucharist, the outward forms and inner meaning of which became established as precious symbolic elements in medieval story. The Sacred Vessel, therefore, is not pagan in origin. Waite acknowledges, however, that it received coloring from non-Christian myth. Except for its sacramental side it is "Celtic on the surface and Celtic also in atmosphere."[16] But he maintains that these are the least significant elements in the story, the core of which continues to be the mystery of a Secret Doctrine and a Reliquary Legend.

Waite also makes observations on the characteristics of the Grail legend which have a direct bearing on the work of Machen and Williams. First he stresses the poignant sense of deprivation in the withholding or the removal of the Grail from human sight. The story of the Holy Vessel, he says, is a "very melancholy Legend; it is the passing of a Great Procession and a Great Sacrament, which . . . is destined never to return in the same form: it is a portion of the loss of humanity on one side of its manhood."[17] Moreover, he emphasizes the dark curse which fell upon the land of Logres because of errors of omission at the Grail Castle. Of the *Perlesvaus* he says, in a way which suggests Williams' manner of thinking, "When the enemy of the Laws of Light entered into the Hidden House of God, the Chapel of the Holy Grail was emptied of its Hallows, which were taken into deeper retreat."[18] Further, Waite holds that in striving for union with the Grail one should be guided not so much by ethics as by mystical sensitivity. The Perceval story describes the disastrous results when a certain question is not asked. The needful thing is to *ask*, whereupon one receives. This problem comes to the fore in the imperfectly understood character of Galahad, who should not — Tennyson to the contrary notwithstanding — be conceived largely as an ethical force. As one immediately infused with Divine Grace he "dissolved temptation, as one more than human."[19] The dedicated spirit needs no elaborate code of conduct: "There is nothing in the world which has less to do with a process or other conventions and artifices than the ascent of a soul to light. Thus, the Quest has no formulae."[20] The confident simplicity of Archdeacon Davenant in Williams' *War in Heaven* comes to mind as we read this passage. Finally, Waite tries to describe the sublime mystery of the Grail's presence. He tells us of the hermit in the *Grand Saint Graal*, who, after reading in a precious book given him by the "Grand Master," is transported to the Third Heaven, where at last he comes to a perfect understanding of the Trinity. The Grail, says Waite, "has the music of all the plain song of all the masses and high *Epiclesis* clauses; and behind it is the music, as it seems to me, of yet another Mass, which we would give our souls to hear; but it has not been drawn as yet into the Liturgy of any known Church."[21] Thus in a number of ways the new departures of Machen and Williams in Grail fiction had been anticipated in Waite.[22]

In his novel *The Secret Glory* (1922), Arthur Machen makes his most ambitious attempt to describe the mystery and the spiritual power of the Grail. As in "The Great Return" the action takes place in Machen's own Britain; the reader is not transported to a medieval nowhere. It is a strange, discursive story of a young Welshman, Ambrose Meyrick, and his achieving of the Grail. Revolting against the athleticism and the synthetic "school spirit" of Lupton School, where he is a student and of which his uncle is second in command, Meyrick runs away with a housemaid in his final year. Convinced after a short time that he is on the wrong track he leaves her, and the main body of the story ends.

The Grail plays a large part in the story. Years before, when Meyrick was a boy, his father had helped him develop a love of Celtic lore, particularly in relation to the early Church. Together they visited holy places in Wales. On one occasion his father took him to the house of the farmer, Cradock, who by long unbroken succession had become Keeper of the Hallows. There the Grail appeared in all its splendor. Meyrick's whole life was colored by this experience, and his revolt against Lupton and his elopement with the housemaid were indications of a passionate though ill-directed quest. The main body of the story ends with his aim still unfulfilled. An Epilogue, however, gathers together the fragmentary reports of his last adventures. On the death of Cradock he succeeded to the keepership of the Grail and undertook to transport it to a secret shrine in Asia where it would be forever hidden. While returning to Europe he was captured by wild Turkish or Kurdish tribesmen and crucified. Thus he achieved the "Red Martyrdom" foretold by an old fiddler of his school days at Lupton, as well as "the most glorious Quest and Adventure of the Sangraal."

As a novel *The Secret Glory* has many weaknesses. In the first place, it is divided in aim. Machen cannot decide whether to write a savage satire against the English Public School system or a tale of supernatural glory. The two do not mix happily. Moreover, Meyrick is too erratic to win sympathy. He has more than a little intellectual snobbery, and a hysterical restlessness which does not suit the supreme champion of the Grail. Also, the story is poorly constructed. The achieving of the Grail through the adventure in Asia is told only as an afterthought in the Epilogue. Yet in spite of its weaknesses *The Secret Glory* deserves a place in any account of the modern Grail legend because Machen insists on the sacramental character of the old story, and because at his best he writes with imaginative power.

In his essay "Celtic Magic" Machen emphasizes the sense of deprivation which gives tragic force to the story of the Grail. "It seems to me [he says] that it is the sense of a great loss which lies at the root of all Celtic magic, the Celtic mysticism, the Celtic wonder." And again: "The whole legend of the Graal is a tale of a great and woeful loss.... The Holy Vessel was withdrawn from Britain by reason of the wickedness of the Britons."[23] This point is also stressed further in his collection of essays, *The Glorious Mystery* (1924). Machen mentions the removal of the Grail to the realm of Prester John in Wolfram von Eschenbach's *Parzival*, and speaks of the dire enchantment under which Logres languishes because of the blindness of men.[24] These conditions, in slightly varied form, underlie the tension of *The Secret Glory*. Meyrick's whole world is blighted by the stupidity of those who should see clearly; the springs of intellectual and spiritual insight are dried at the source. The very Grail itself is kept closely concealed in the place where one might least expect to find it, and finally is permanently removed to the remote fastnesses of Asia.

Yet for those who can see, the Holy Vessel is blindingly immediate and ineffably comforting. In *The Glorious Mystery* Machen speaks of what the Grail hero will experience:

His are the delights that are almost unendurable, the wonders that are almost incredible — that are, indeed, quite incredible to the world; his the eternal joys that the deadly flesh cannot comprehend; his the secret that renews the earth, restoring Paradise, rolling the heavy stone of the material universe from the grave whence he arises.[25]

Meyrick realizes these joys to the full, not only in an early vision of the Chapel of the Grail, but also and more especially in his experience at the house of the Keeper, Cradock. "Bliss possessed him utterly" as he gazed at the richness of the Cup, intricately wrought of gold and silver and copper and bronze, and flaming with jewels that seemed to emit "a shower of glittering stars." Ecstatically there arose in his mind a vision of the sacred city, Corarbennic:

It seemed to him that, for a moment of time, he saw in unendurable light the Mystery of Mysteries pass veiled before him, and the Image of the Slain and Risen. For a brief while this dream was broken. He heard his father singing softly: "Gogoniant y Tâd ac y Mab ac yr Yspryd Glân." And the old man answered: "Agya Trias eleeson ymas." Then again his spirit was lost in the bright depths of the crystal, and he saw the ships of the saints, without oar or sail, afloat on the faery sea, seeking the Glassy Isle. All the whole company of the Blessed Saints of the Isle of Britain sailed on the adventure; dawn and sunset, night and morning, their illumined faces never wavered; and Ambrose thought that at last they saw bright shores in the dying light of a red sun, and there came to their nostrils the scent of the deep apple-garths in Avalon, and odours of Paradise.[26]

In this passage and others like it, all charged with Celtic imagination, Machen sees the Grail at the heart of the eucharistic mystery. It is true that he does so emphasizing Cymric wonder as well as Christian doctrine,[27] but the important fact is that he did it at all, and as effectively as he did. There remained only for Williams to add his deep understanding of theology and his picture of the great struggle between good and evil to infuse the legend of the Grail and the "Tragedy of Camelot" with meaning never before achieved in Arthurian literature.

In passing from Machen to Williams, one should remember an elusive but important point. Critics and readers have attacked the otherworldly aloofness of the Grail hero. In *The Arthur of the English Poets* (1907), Howard Maynadier chides Tennyson for his picture of Galahad, whom he calls "unhuman and unnatural." In *The Glorious Mystery* (p. 53) Machen objects. After dealing with Maynadier's statement he goes on to say that the writer of great romance "must be firmly and utterly convinced that man is here, not that he may be good-natured and kindly (so far as kindness and good nature are consistent with business principles) but that he may be worthy of the Vision of the Most Blessed Cup of the Sangraal." Ethics as ethics, therefore, is not a necessary part of the Grail story; the hero is not following a code of conduct; he is the instrument of Divine Grace. Just as the Grail is independent of formal ethics so also is it independent of place and time. It can appear anywhere, at any moment. In "Modernism," one of the essays in *The Glorious Mystery,* Machen tells of a pious woman who opened a richly decorated chapel in western London, and uses the illustration to prove an important point — one which helps to explain the modern setting of Williams' *War in Heaven:* "Even in modern 'civilized' London the Quest of the Sangraal is not impossible." Thus the Quest becomes an immediate, possible actuality, a search which continues through all ages. It is no longer an adventure reserved to the knights of chivalry. In mysterious and even what might seem accidental ways the Grail can reappear in modern Britain.

Charles Williams probably knew Machen's Arthurian writings. In "The Figure of Arthur," the unfinished history of the Arthurian legend published in *Arthurian Torso* (1948), he makes a footnote reference to Waite. Remembering Waite's friendship with Machen and the allusions to him in *The Holy Grail,* it certainly seems likely that Williams would have tracked Machen down. Whether he did or not, however, is beside the point. The fact is that Williams carried to brilliant heights what Machen had begun. He did so because he was both an extraordinarily devoted Christian and a thoughtful scholar, and because he released an imaginative invention seldom surpassed in the Arthurian story.

Some day — and his admirers hope it will be soon — Charles Williams' power as an author will be made plain by a systematic study of all his works. When he died unexpectedly in 1945 he was still in middle age, yet in a relatively short life he wrote much, in drama, criticism, theology, fiction, and poetry. A great deal of this was done in time stolen from his work as one of the staff of the Oxford University Press. Yet a hard-won creativity never dulled his keenness (it appears

in vivid flashes even in works he frankly thought of as pot-
boilers), and never altered the soundness and grace of mind
which still keep his memory fresh among his friends at Oxford.
Widely read, particularly in theology and literature,[28] he suggests Coleridge in the breadth and grasp of his mind and in
the darting play of his thought. Yet in other ways, in his
humility and his stability of character, he was as unlike the
other as possible.

In 1930, Williams took his place in the first rank of modern
Arthurians with *War in Heaven,* the most deeply moving piece
of prose fiction to spring from the legend in modern times,
and a triumphant realization of the possibilities already foreshadowed in the work of Arthur Machen.

The struggle in the book is the ancient one. In Revelation
12:7-12 we read:

There was war in heaven: Michael and his angels fought
against the dragon; and the dragon fought and his angels,
and prevailed not; neither was their place found any more
in heaven. . . . Therefore, rejoice, ye heavens, and ye that dwell
in them. Woe to the inhabiters of the earth and of the sea!
for the devil is come down unto you, having great wrath,
because he knoweth that he hath but a short time.

Yet though heaven and hell come to grips in Williams'
novel, they do so on earth, in a quiet British village and at
the present time. From a passing remark in an archaeological
work about to be published, Archdeacon Davenant, vicar of
Fardles, discovers that an ancient chalice in his church is the
Holy Graal. This fact also becomes known to the publisher of
the book, Gregory Persimmons, who has long been interested
in black magic. It soon becomes evident that he is a part of
satanic schemes to capture and destroy the Graal. There fol-

lows a series of swift adventures, in which the excitement of the best detective fiction is shot through with diabolical incantation on the one side and Christian faith on the other. The Graal falls into the hands of the enemy, Persimmons and his superiors: the Greek Dimitri, who operates a dingy chemist's shop in London, and the old Jew, Manasseh. The shadow of unimaginable disaster looms over the guardians of the sacred vessel, and indeed over the Christian cosmos. In this moment of mortal danger there appears a mysterious young man, later revealed as Prester John, the guardian of the Graal and the very embodiment of it. Through his intervention, a young woman driven mad by Persimmons' magic is saved from damnation, and Archdeacon Davenant, whose soul the evil forces are on the point of degrading by union with that of a commonplace murdered man, is rescued to the crashing chorus of a celestial litany. The book closes with the celebration of the Mass of the Graal in the church at Fardles. At the end of the service both Prester John, the celebrant, and the Graal disappear; the Archdeacon dies on the sanctuary steps.

Within the relatively brief compass of the 256 pages of *War in Heaven* there lies a whole world of excitement, physical, emotional, and spiritual. Probably never before in Grail literature had the issues of conflict been more vividly presented.

This conflict helps to distinguish Williams' novel from earlier works, chiefly those of Arthur Machen. In Machen the supremacy of the Grail is an established fact; its position is threatened only by the blindness of men and not by satanic power. Therefore, its eucharistic function is almost solely that of revealing hitherto uncomprehended Grace. *War in Heaven*, on the other hand, emphasizes the spiritual conflict found in the Bible and Milton; the devil strives desperately on earth "because he knoweth that he hath but a short time." In the

war against evil, the Grail becomes a living symbol of unleashed spiritual power, its force lying not only in its essence,
but also in its dynamic capacity.

The story is filled with the tension of conflict on a universal
scale; the enemies of the Grail are fully determined to bring
about the reign of chaos. Manasseh is the voice of his satanic
superiors when he says to Dimitri and Persimmons: "To destroy this [the Graal] is to ruin another of their houses, and
another step towards the hour when we shall breathe against
the heavens and they shall fall."[29] With high excitement,
Williams describes Persimmons' attempt to destroy the sacred
vessel by remote control while it is being guarded in London
by the Archdeacon and his friends Kenneth Mornington and
the Duke of the North Ridings. As the Cup quivers and trem-
bles in Davenant's hands, now seeming to soften and now to
harden, he calls upon his companions to "pray that He who
made the universe may sustain the universe, that in all things
there may be delight in the justice of His will."[30] Then follows
a time in which the three Grail champions — Mornington earlier having referred to himself as Bors, the Duke as Percivale,
and the Archdeacon as Galahad — undergo a kind of psychological and spiritual siege. None of the customary ghosts or
diabolical phantoms appear; horror is suggested by sudden
and inexplicable hints of malign power beating against them,
in the half-caught sound of a footstep or a whisper, and in
Mornington's moments of weakness and self-justification. Eventually the strength of Davenant pulls them through; his aware-
ness of the scope and purpose of the struggle provides the
saving flash of insight, and the Graal is secure for the time
being.

The supreme danger, however, is yet to come, and with it,
the most moving projection of Williams' dark fantasy. The

Archdeacon lies bound in the chemist's shop with the Graal on his chest, and Persimmons tries, with the power of the Cup and his own satanic rites, to fuse Davenant's soul with that of the murdered Pattison. It is a scene of great horror, for it is spiritual degradation and not physical danger which threatens the Archdeacon. Moreover, the fate of the Christian world is bound up with Davenant's; terrible forces are at work:

This procession [of powers flowing from Persimmons] was not alone; it was controlled and directed by mightier powers. From another centre there issued a different force, and this, the victim realized, it would need all his present strength to meet. There impinged upon him the knowledge of all hateful and separating and deathly things: madness and tormenting disease and the vengeance of gods. This was the hunger with which creation preys upon itself, a supernatural famine that has no relish except for the poisons that waste it. This was the second death that cannot die, and it ran actively through that world of immortalities on a hungry mission of death.

Against the pulverizing nihilism which beats upon him, Davenant clings to himself, and suddenly, through his own strength and that of a greater than he — Prester John — the spell is broken:

The faint glow around the Vessel faded and vanished; and all the moving darkness of the room seemed to direct itself towards and to emerge from that thickest core of night which beat in the Cup, as if its very heart were beating there. One moment only they heard and felt that throbbing heart, and then suddenly from it there broke a terrific and golden light; blast upon blast of trumpets shook the air; the Graal blazed with fiery tumult before them; and its essence, as at last that essence was touched, awoke in its own triumphant and blinding power. None could tell whether light and trumpets were

162

indeed there; but something was there — something which, as it caught and returned upon them the energies they had put forth, seemed also to bestride the prostrate figure on the floor. The Graal was lifted or was itself no more — they could not tell; they were flung back before this lifting and visible form. He over whom it stood returned also from the depths; he looked up and saw it flaming through the scattering night, and heard a litany which changed as it smote his ears from the chant of an unknown tongue into the familiar and cherished maxims of his natural mind.

"Let them give thanks whom the Lord hath redeemed," a great voice sang, and from all about it, striking into light and sound at once, the answer came: "for His mercy endureth for ever."[31]

The battle is won. All that remains is the translation of Prester John and the Graal after the service at Fardles and the gentle death of the Archdeacon.

Davenant's gentle death is entirely fitting, not only as catharsis in the story but also because it closes the career of the Grail hero in the simple confidence he should always show. Like Galahad, the Archdeacon makes no demands. He asks for nothing because he has everything; yet having everything, again like Galahad, he lives in an aura of transparent humility. Reverence is perhaps not the right word for it; Davenant's every action is directed by a kind of grave and even sedate courtesy toward both man and God.

"Ah, fair sweet Lord," he said half-aloud [as he held the Graal], "let me keep this, Thy vessel, if it be Thy vessel; for love's sake, fair Lord, if Thou hast held it in Thy hands, let me take it into mine. And, if not, let me be courteous still to it for Thy sake, courteous Lord; since this might well have been that, and that was touched by Thee."[32]

It goes without saying that the Archdeacon is more real as a person than Galahad. The earlier Grail hero is a spiritual personification, less man than extension of the Divine Presence. Davenant, on the other hand, is very much a man, and this not merely because he happens to be living in our own time. Essentially the difference between the two seems to lie in the degree of conscious dedication. From the very beginning Galahad is born to a mission. Prophecies of his unique character and position abound; the Siege Perilous awaits him at Arthur's Table. The Archdeacon, on the contrary, is a simple country priest, as unaware of the great role he is to play as anyone about him. Though his purity of heart is a sign of unusual rewards of God's grace, he never seems superhuman. He is saved from the stiffness of spiritual symbolism by his wit, his common sense, and his modest expectations. In this last respect, he has what Keats called "negative capability," that is, an acceptance of all that life means of good or ill without an irritable reaching out after fact or reason. Finally, it is a high tribute to him as a character when we say that he helps to make credible the incredible.

There is probably a good deal of Charles Williams himself in Archdeacon Davenant, and this not simply because of the unself-conscious grace of the two. For Williams could not have convinced us of the incredible unless he had been sure, like the Archdeacon, that heaven and hell are closer to us than we ever imagine. As a matter of fact, Williams believed that the natural and the supernatural world are one and indivisible; he moved as easily and as naturally in one as in the other. T. S. Eliot makes this point clearly in one of his essays. He speaks of Williams' "extra perceptiveness," his "extended spiritual sense." And he continues wittily:

At ease in human society, I am sure that he would have remained equally composed if a ghost, an angel, or an evil spirit had entered the room. He would have known how to receive any kind of supernatural visitor. If I had ever had to spend a night in a haunted house, I should have felt fearless with Charles Williams in my company.[33]

This familiarity with other worlds is a vital part of Williams' strength as a writer, for it places him at the center of a world of events and issues hardly dreamt of in our philosophy. Within this larger world Williams moves confidently, meeting its problems with mental and emotional elasticity. This confidence is particularly clear in his attitude toward evil. In the article already mentioned, T. S. Eliot says of him, "He was not puritanical, because he was not frightened by evil." This is not to say that he minimized it. To him evil is a spiritual reality; it is not caused by a dislocation of genes or hormones or by a set of psychopathic fixations. It is a gigantic negative force aimed at the reduction of the cosmos ordained by the Divine Will, and it operates through the degradation of fallible human beings. Yet the man who knows what it is and who tries to understand God's grace, as Williams did, can not be injured or paralyzingly frightened by it. He will seek to understand it more and more, the better to combat it.

War in Heaven brings evil before the reader in a frightening way. It would be hard to forget the scene in which Persimmons leagues himself with sinister powers. Yet as always, Williams does not rely on melodrama; the whole episode is underwritten, and the usual apparatus of diabolical compacts is completely missing. The author simply wishes to understand as fully as possible what is happening, both inwardly and outwardly, as Persimmons applies the satanic ointment. What is happening terrifies the reader more than it does the author, for to him, good and evil are both essentially simple. He believes that if they are approached with this conviction fearlessly, the one can be exalted and the other cast down.

The Graal is the instrument of victory in this gigantic conflict — a development virtually unique in the history of the legend. The eucharistic significance of the Cup had been restored by Arthur Machen, yet it remained for Williams to make it a weapon of universal power. This means a certain shift in emphasis: the Sacred Vessel is not simply to be sought and found, but rather to be *preserved* against an onslaught undreamed of by the Fisher-King. The ancestral voices prophesying war in our age of global conflict and spiritual skepticism sound loud and clear in *War in Heaven*.

The ancestral voices are heard again in Charles Williams' poems, in which he leaves the England of his own experience and turns to Arthur's Britain. These poems appear in three collections: *Three Plays* (1931), which includes five incidental Arthurian verses, and *Taliessin Through Logres* (1938) and *The Region of the Summer Stars* (1944), which deal wholly with the legend.

The songs in *Three Plays* are very different poems from those in the other two volumes, for the Taliessin who sings them sees few of the theological and legendary mysteries which moved him later. The early pieces are only the first intimations of spirituality. As in Williams' later poems, Taliessin, the Welsh seer, is appalled by the chaos of Logres before the coming of Arthur, and goes to the Emperor in Byzantion for aid and comfort. Then follows the triumphant crowning of the King. Yet the Grail, which is the *raison d'être* of Williams' Arthuriad, is mentioned only obliquely in the song which describes Galahad's ceremonious installation in King Arthur's bed. Occasionally in these poems, however, one finds Williams' authentic power. In "Taliessin's Song of Logres" universal disaster sweeps around us:

> Loosed are the powers of earth and air,
> fire and water in combat leap;
> space is now but a broken stair,
> and the great sun runs on the edge of a steep
> dizzy with terror; for all around
> the elementals again abound
> in clamour and freedom; water, fire,
> earth and air unprison their powers,
> and no prayer reacheth the heavenly Sire
> where he sitteth calm in his lucid towers.[34]

And the account of Galahad's stately bedding has the imaginative grasp of the Grail hero's unique position which is the shining center of the later poems. Even so, the songs in *Three Plays* are inferior to *Taliessin Through Logres* and *The Region of the Summer Stars*. True, they are easier to understand and are more traditional in the use of meter and rhyme. What they chiefly lack is the full sweep of Williams' imagination; that was to come abundantly before very long. Father Gervase Mathew, one of his close friends, writes interestingly of his growth:

He had become increasingly sacramental in his attitude towards material things. During his last years there was a curiously incandescent quality both in what he wrote and what he was; in teaching, writing and friendship he had gained the power first to illuminate and then by that illumination to perceive.[35]

It is important to remember that Williams had a double advantage as an Arthurian. He was a scholar as well as a man of vaulting, illuminative imagination. His friends were struck by the breadth and depth of his knowledge. C. S. Lewis writes:

Though not a professional scholar, [he was] one of the best informed of us all and will always stand in my mind as a cheering proof of how far a man can go with few languages and imperfect schooling. On the ancients and on the early Middle Ages there were one or two present with whom he could not compete, nor had he an exact knowledge of any of the great philosophers: but in history, theology, legend, comparative religion, and (above all) English literature from Shakespeare down, his knowledge was surprising.[36]

He came to the Arthurian legend not only as a creator but also as a scholar, as witness his unfinished history of the cycle, "The Figure of Arthur," and his article, "Malory and the Grail Legend" (*Dublin Review*, 1944). His studies gave him a grasp of the Grail legend and its deep implications which helped him immeasurably.

The poems in *Taliessin Through Logres* and *The Region of the Summer Stars* comprise parts of an uncompleted Arthurian cycle. A brief summary will serve to outline the general pattern.[37]

The infant Taliessin is rescued from a coracle floating down the river Wye by Elphin, son of Gwyddno, and grows up in Elphin's household. His association with otherworldly experience is early evident, for his "true region is the summer stars."[38] In his youth he hears talk of "the Empire" and of Christianity, and in the course of exploratory travels comes to the wood of Broceliande. There live Merlin and Brisen, son and daughter of Nimue; beyond is the place of the Hallows, Pelles' sacred kingdom of Carbonek; over the sea farther west lies the holy city of Sarras; in the antipodes and yet contiguous to the wood is the dark, slimy land of P'o-l'u, the edge of Hell.

Merlin, who with his sister is charged with establishing in Logres a realm like that of Carbonek, sends Taliessin to Byzantium, the seat of the Christian Empire. There he has an interview with the Emperor, who probably represents perception of God, after which he returns to Britain dedicated to the idea of uniting Broceliande and all of Logres with Byzantium. Meanwhile Arthur, with Merlin's help, comes to power in the torn and famished land. King Cradlemas, the last decadent remnant of Roman power, is overcome, and after the great victory over the Saxons at Mount Badon (in which Taliessin plays a soldierly part), Arthur is crowned King. Thus the temporal realm is established. The spiritual realm, as in Malory, takes its course to a dark and tragic (but by no means hopeless) end, made inevitable by man's godlike vision and his fallibility.

The story is not told in clear narrative sequence; the reader has to assemble details from highly allusive and elliptical passages. Even so we see the divisive, destructive forces at work: Morgause of Orkney, hewn from northern stone, beloved of Lamorack and the mother of Arthur's incestuous son; Palomides the Saracen, whose love for Iseult leads him into barren caves of thought and the fruitless search for the Questing Beast; Lancelot, the strength of Arthur's right arm, and the unwitting agent, in his son Galahad, of spiritual triumph, yet with Guinevere, the agent of disaster; finally Mordred, calmly and cynically plotting the overthrow of his father's kingdom. Others work for the spiritual land of Logres. Merlin makes it possible for Galahad to be conceived, and Taliessin founds a "Company," springing up almost spontaneously among all sorts and conditions of trustful people, whose "cult was the Trinity and the Flesh-taking." Bors, Percivale and his sister Dindrane, and Galahad see the promise of "the Empire" clearly; Galahad realizes the dream fully in himself. Yet the supreme irony ensues: the Grail champion sails to the holy city of Sarras, and the Sacred Vessel vanishes from Logres. The cycle ends as the Pope in Rome, appalled by the disaster in Britain, prays for God's grace; Lancelot devoutly sings the Mass.

From this summary it will be evident that in general Williams holds to the traditional outline of the story.[39] Within that outline, however, the treatment is brilliantly individual. In fact *Taliessin Through Logres* and *The Region of the Summer Stars* stand alone in the long record of Arthurian literature. And it is not enough merely to say that Williams places the sacramental Grail at the heart of the story. Others had done that before him. Seldom if ever before, however, had it been done with such imaginative power. Williams' serene belief in divine mysteries, even in the face of monstrous evil, gives daring and exciting expansiveness to the poems. The universe and our world become one; human experience is harmonized and interpenetrated by the miraculous.

First there is the concept of the Empire, a region whose physical boundaries are roughly those of the Romano-Byzantine imperium, whose spiritual boundaries are the vastness of God's grace. Recognizing the interdependence of flesh and spirit, Williams sometimes conceives of it as a human body: Logres is (or is to be) the brain, Gaul the breasts, Rome the hands. Byzantium, the physical center of the body (just as it was the seat of the Roman Empire in Arthur's day), is also the spiritual center, and the Emperor, while not in the conventional sense a symbol of God, represents something like the vision of divinity. His realm is one of stylized and yet perfectly natural order:

> *The Empire lay in the imposed order; around*
> *the Throne the visionary zone of clear light*

hummed with celestial action; there the forms
of chamberlains, logothetes, nuncios, went and came,
diagrams of light moving in the light.[40]

In the antipodes, touching on Byzantium (and also by a daring leap of the imagination on Broceliande) lay the dark land of P'o-l'u, where order is denied or perverted:

> *Those*
> *who worked in the ports heard shipmen say*
> *that in the antipodean ocean was a sight*
> *known only to the Emperor's lordliest admirals*
> *who, closeliest obeying command, passed*
> *near to the harbour and vile marshes of P'o-l'u;*
> *there on the waves a headless Emperor walked*
> *coped in a foul indecent crimson; octopods*
> *round him stretched giant tentacles and crawled*
> *heavily on the slimy surface of the tangled sea,*
> *goggling with lidless eyes at the coast of the Empire.*[41]

Broceliande is more difficult to understand than Byzantium. To many people it is dark and dangerous, yet it is luminous with the twin figures of Merlin and Brisen, and the light which shines upon Nimue from the third heaven. In this forest, gigantic, inchoate forces are in flux, not in the sense of good at war with evil but rather in the struggle of forms to emerge. Nimue is the power which translates ideal, heavenly prototypes into actuality; her children Merlin and Brisen (called Time and Space by Williams) do her work in trying to bring the divine order of the Empire to Logres. Williams' imagination soars to the third heaven itself in a passage of sweeping metaphysical suggestion:

> *Done was the day; the antipodean sun*
> *cast earth's coned shadow into space;*

it exposed the summer stars; as they rose
the light of Taliessin's native land
shone in a visible glory over him sleeping.
Rarely through the wood rang a celestial cry,
sometimes with a like reply, sometimes with none.
The trees shook, in no breeze, to a passage of power.
Under the ground was the sound of great waves
breaking round huge caves, ancient sepulchres,
where Ocean, a young child of making, held
talk with the first mother of making, Nimue:–

. . . . . .

The cone's shadow of earth fell into space,
and into (other than space) the third heaven.
In the third heaven are the living unriven truths,
climax tranquil in Venus. Merlin and Brisen
heard, as in faint bee-like humming
round the cone's point, the feeling intellect hasten
to fasten on the earth's image; in the third heaven
the stones of the waste glimmered like summer stars.[42]

The actors in Williams' cycle move in a world interfused with heaven, a world in which the redemption of Man from his fall is to be achieved through the Holy Vessel of God. The Grail stands at the very center of the work,[43] and never before had it done so with more originality, even though it is virtually unrevealed. Whereas Malory brought the Sacred Vessel before our very eyes in Arthur's hall and in Launcelot's inner room of ordeal, Williams conceives of the Grail as an idea or a presence, an emanation of the Divine Order. The enemies of Light fail to perceive this sanctity: Balin the Savage, who impiously wounds King Pelles with the Dolorous Blow; Palomides, whose love for Iseult furrows itself into concupiscence and whose final christening is almost an act of quiet desperation; indeed Lancelot himself, whose sin with Guinevere is only dangerously redeemed. Mordred, the worst of all the destroyers (his "realistic," cynical mind leaves no room for either passion or compassion), is guilty of a heresy that has dogged the Grail from the Middle Ages right down to our own day. He says:

> *My father dwelled on the thought of the Grail for his luck,*
> *but I can manage without such fairy mechanism.*[44]

The Grail is no "fairy mechanism" to Williams, and it is not a chivalric proving ground. It is the supreme symbol of God's compact with Man at the Table of the Last Supper. The Quest is therefore elevated by the extraordinary devotion of man to man and man to God. Though this is no innovation in the legend, Williams gives the Grail adventure entirely fresh meaning by his devout, original treatment.

This is a remarkable achievement when we consider that the actors in the story are not "characters" in the ordinary sense of the word; one might say they were abstractions if the word did not imply a close identification with a single virtue rather than a complex and elastic spiritual situation. They are seen in action little and their adventures follow anything but the stock chivalric pattern. The poems are reflections on (or of) characters acutely sensitized to otherworldly influences. Yet Williams' people are not unreal. In spite of ellipticality which makes the poems far from easy reading, in spite of Williams' unconventional method of characterization, his people are individuals. Each person in the story is seen in an enlarged frame of reality, his own actions but the outward (and least important) element in the supernatural relationship which gives him his reason for being.

The doctrine of reciprocity between two worlds, which Williams develops into an elaborate theological pattern beyond the scope of this book,[45] helps to make his characters persons rather than abstractions, and, what is more, gives the best of them a serene sense of balance. In his play *The House of the Octopus* (1949, p. 111) Williams makes a statement which goes to the root of the matter. The Marshal of an invading force from P'o-l'u is describing the difference between his people and the conquered Christians:

> *There is one choice everywhere —*
> *even between us, Prefect, —*
> *and that is to be*
> *the swallowed or the swallower. I have heard say*
> *that these Christians pretend an and enters —*
> *swallow and be swallowed, consume and be consumed.*
> *That is folly.*

The people of P'o-l'u hold to a rigid "either-or" position; the Christians (remembering that God became Man and that Man became God) hold to the reality of interchange between the human and divine.

This belief gives an unself-conscious decorum to Williams' world. It acounts for his spontaneous and unsensual recognition of delight in body as well as spirit (notice particularly the frisking naked girls in Caucasus) and for the translucent humility of those who work for the union of Byzantium and Logres. Neither way of life, the ascetic or the romantic, is sufficient unto itself. There is a constant interplay between the two, a constant recognition of the rights of others less gifted. So Dindrane, the sister of Percivale, gives her blood and her life for a sick lady, and Taliessin imparts wisdom to all kinds of men in his "Company." Especially we remember Galahad. Malory (Bk. XVII) reminds us of his filial love: "My fayre lorde [says Galahad to Bors], salew me unto my lorde Sir Launcelot, my fadir, and as sone as ye se hym bydde hym remembir of this worlde unstable." True to his doctrine of interchange Williams gives new force to the relation of father and son. Galahad's earthly love is no less strong because he has his eyes fixed on the Grail. His love is all the greater because he realizes that his very existence has brought untold suffering to Lancelot. All this becomes clear as Percivale and Galahad stand before the Castle of Carbonek:

> *In the rent saffron sun hovered the Grail.*
> *Galahad stood in the arch of Carbonek;*
> *the people of Pelles ran to meet him.*
> *His eyes were sad; he sighed for Lancelot's pardon.*
>
> *Joy remembered joylessness; joy kneeled*
> *under the arch where Lancelot ran in frenzy.*
> *The astonished angels of the spirit heard him moan:*
> *Pardon, lord; pardon and bless me, father.*
>
> . . . . . .
>
> *Under the arch the Merciful Child*
> *wept for the grief of his father in reconciliation;*
> *who was betrayed there by Merlin and Brisen*
> *to truth; he saw not; he was false to Guinevere.*[46]

Galahad's sorrow for his father is all the greater because he realizes that the doctrine of reciprocity can work both ways: interchange is possible not only with the powers of light but also the powers of darkness. A substitution divinely ordained puts Helayne,[47] the daughter of King Pelles, in Guinevere's place. Galahad is conceived on the night of her meeting with Lancelot. Yet the remorse for his misdeed, increased by the shock of deception, forces Lancelot into a *sinister* substitution: "he [runs] into a delirium of lycanthropy" and turns into a great grey wolf.

All the winter the wolf haunted the environs of Carbonek;
now what was left of the man's contrarious mind
was twinned and twined with the beast's bent to feed;
now it crept to swallow the seed
of love's ambiguity, love's taunt and truth.
Man, he hated; beast, he hungered; both
stretched his sabres and strained his throat; rumble
of memories of love in the gaunt belly told
his instinct only that something edible might come.
Slavering he crouched by the dark arch of Carbonek,
head-high howling, lusting for food, living
for flesh, a child's flesh, his son's flesh.

Guinevere, sleeping, grasps the full terror of what has happened:

The queen's tormented unaesthetic womanhood
alternately wept and woke, her sobs crushed
deep as the winter howls were high, her limbs
swathed by tentacles, her breasts sea-weighed.
Across the flat sea she saw Lancelot
walking, a grotesque back, the opposite of a face
looking backward like a face; she burst the swollen sea
shrieking his name; nor he turned nor looked,
but small on the level dwindled to a distant manikin,
the tinier the more terrible, the sole change
in her everlastingness, except, as Merlin passed,
once as time passed, the hoary waters
laughed backward in her mouth and drowned her tongue.[48]

One would have to look long and hard to find a passage in which blind, unreasoning delirium and fear play so large a part in the estrangement of the lovers. By this dramatic device, Williams makes Lancelot's final victory over himself almost unimaginably brave, and he makes completely credible the pity and even anguish which rushes over Galahad, the son.

Yet though Galahad can feel as a man, he lives in his own divine world. The Grail disappears from Logres, but not from the sight of the Grail hero; his achievement gives catharsis to Williams' cycle and keeps alive the hope of otherwise hopeless men. The sharp edge of sound from celestial trumpets seems to fill the air as Galahad sails to Sarras. It is not a Wagnerian salute in brass; it is not the chiding of Keats's "silver snarling trumpets." There is nothing "romantic" in the music we seem to hear; it is stately, yet full of light and movement, stylized yet graceful, orderly without constriction. As it first strikes the ear it may sound disharmonic, but as we listen again and recall the themes from which it springs, we seem to catch the music of the spheres:

An infinite flight of doves from the storming sky
of Logres — strangely sea-travellers when the land melts —
forming to overfeather and overwhelm the helm,
numerous as men in the empire, the empire riding
the skies of the ocean, guiding by modulated stresses
on each spoke of the helm the vessel from the realm of Arthur,
lifted oak and elm to a new-ghosted power.
The hosted wings trapped the Infant's song;
blown back, tossed down, thrown
along the keel, the song hastening the keel
along the curve of the sea-way, the helm fastening
the whole ship to the right balance of the stresses;

. . . . . .

Through the sea of omnipotent fact rushed the act of Galahad.
He glowed white; he leaned against the wind
down the curved road among the topless waters.
He sang Judica te, Deus; *the wind,*
driven by doves' wings along the arm-taut keel,
sang against itself Judica te, Deus.

Prayer and irony had said their say and ceased;
the sole speech was speed.
In the hollow of Jerusalem the quadrilateral of the sun
was done on the deck beyond Broceliande.
In the monstrum of triangular speed,
in a path of lineal necessity,
the necessity of being was communicated to the son of
  Lancelot.
The ship and the song drove on.[49]

Williams' poems brilliantly illustrate the experimental, re-constructive temper of the best modern Arthurians. From the old legend, which he knew well as a scholar, he extracted the spiritual core; on this basis he developed a profoundly religious cycle. His originality both in conception and style is amazing, so much so that readers of his poems will doubtless have trouble with symbolism and expression which sometimes baffle even C. S. Lewis, his friend and commentator. It is not every-one, as Edna St. Vincent Millay discovered, who can easily apprehend "light anatomized." Yet there is a world of differ-ence between Williams and some of the other cryptic poets of our time, between the obscurity which conceals the common-place and that which shadows forth vast cloudy symbols. In Williams the epic proportions of the legend have been ex-tended far beyond Malory's concept of a collapsing temporal kingdom. The scope is now Miltonic; the struggle primarily concerns man's responsibility under divine law. The two worlds of heaven and earth become one. And if in fusing them into transcendental reality Williams leads us into a third heaven which we never made, we should remember that out of the Summer Stars comes the mandate without which human life has no reason for being.

Before we leave the spiritual land of Logres, there are sev-

eral other contemporary writers who deserve attention, three
of them far inferior to Williams, one of them his equal. Like
him, they describe Arthur's kingdom at least in some degree
as a religious battleground. With the exception of C. S. Lewis'
novel, *That Hideous Strength,* one cannot say whether Williams directly influenced any of these works. Possibly the resemblances in general theme (and even in style) spring from
the disturbed curiosity of our time. In any case it is clear that
Williams did not stand alone, at least in Great Britain.

W. P. Ryan's *King Arthur in Avalon* (1934), a poem with
a few flashes of imagination, describes an *Irish* Arthur living
in a western island of Avalon, cut off from England and
Ireland by furies who represent exaggeration of the faults of
chivalry. Though he is pre-Christian, the Sun worship which
he professes somehow foreshadows Christianity. "Christos," for
example, is referred to as "Regent of the Sun." It is Arthur's
function to serve as a tutelary force for those seeking the
divinity of the Christos-Sun. There are occasional reminiscences of Williams, not only in the mystical situation but also
in specific ideas and images. We remember Williams' Merlin,
the seer dedicated to making the order of Byzantium prevail
in Logres, when we hear Ryan's Merlin insist upon "ordered
thinking" in "the spirit's course." In several instances also we
catch hints of Williams' style. The disciple Fergus, for example,
speaks of "the rose of patience fragrant in our hearts." It is not
necessary to suggest that Williams was influenced by Ryan;
the resemblances are probably accidental. All that is needed is
to remark that both authors build on the spiritual foundations
of the legend.

E. S. Padmore's play, *The Death of Arthur* (1936), definitely suggests the tension of conflict between good and evil
so strongly marked in *War in Heaven.* It is not a good play —

179

in fact it is less a play than a series of disjointed, morbid reflections — yet once in a while, wryly and elliptically, it strikes fire. The gist of the story is Arthur's struggle to realize his spiritual strength by rejecting visionary and elusive ideals. In his dying moments, he sees the Grail as a symbol of the innocence of little children. Though this is somewhat obviously and sentimentally handled, elsewhere Padmore reaches a crude kind of power. Mordred is a dark, satanic force in the play, crying out to Merlin:

O, how I hate this sordid, sorry world! For one short hour of perfect bliss I'd shatter it to bits, yea pluck the very stars from heaven and quench them, hissing, in the sea of night.

To which Merlin replies:

Then, passion gratified, once more awaken to primordial form, the so-called chaos of the elements.[50]

Running throughout the play in a series of ill-assorted situations — Vivien, for example, appears as a damsel of the Grail, and Merlin and Mark seem fused in one personality, part seer and part schemer — are premonitions of disaster and moral disillusionment, probably a reflection of the black uncertainty in England and elsewhere before Hitler struck in 1939. Arthur speaks prophetically:

The storm approaches which shall devastate this garden, England, and in devastation purge of its foul atmosphere, for which, as King, we are largely responsible. . . . England's only hope lies in the storm, the ordered fury of the elements.[51]

Ernest Reynolds' *Mephistopheles and the Golden Apples,* published in 1943, that is, after Padmore's prophecy of disaster had become an actuality, also stresses the cosmic conflict between good and evil. A fantastic gallimaufry of visions conjured up by Mephistopheles for Christopher Guntram, a disillusioned Oxford don, including a Hans Christian Andersen fairy tale, the story of Scheherezade, and several Arthurian episodes, Reynolds' poem is a sorry piece of confusion. Yet again the struggle is a religious one; indeed Guntram is finally "saved" before the altar of Christ Church Cathedral, Oxford. In his Preface, the author brings to a head in World War II, the titanic struggle between good and evil so clearly evident in earlier writers. The "present war," he says, shows the "positive cosmic forces of evil constantly clashing with forces of good." And in "Merlin's Pantomime" Galahad cries out:

> *My peace is gone. I once could call*
> *On the Virgin Mother of Christ for strength,...*
> *Now the testimony of Evil shouts me down.*[52]

The testimony of evil as it appears in Reynolds, however, and even in his superiors, Padmore and Ryan, is but fitful heat lightning compared with the storm which breaks in C. S. Lewis' novel, *That Hideous Strength.* This book deserves to be better known than apparently it is. A multitude of readers are aware of Mr. Lewis' brilliant gifts as an interpreter of Christian faith; the fraternity of scholars welcomes him as one of the hierarchy (definitely not the "lowerarchy") of their mystery, yet his gifts as a novelist, especially in the trilogy, *Perelandra, Out of the Silent Planet,* and *That Hideous Strength,* seem somewhat overlooked. The time has come to realize the full extent of his creative faculty. Like his great friend Charles Williams, he reveals in his novels an organic fusion of wide learning and luminous spiritual mythmaking.

His position as Fellow and Tutor of Magdalen College, Oxford, has brought him the rewards of his profession; the dangers of it have passed him by. As this transatlantic traveller can testify, he is the best company imaginable. A superlative talker, he is also a good listener, a point not to be overlooked in one whose ear must catch the sounds of Deep Heaven.

If it were not for the risk of confusion with the fustian of Gothic Romance one could call *That Hideous Strength* a "tale of terror." Certainly it is a terrifying book. Not only literary fashions but man's beliefs in a comfortably stable world have changed out of all recognition since Horace Walpole and Ann Radcliffe sent the shiver up the spine with oratorical ghosts and groans from subterranean vaults. In these days of colossal disaster the devices of the old romances seem amusingly naive, for terror has now been stretched to unimaginable dimensions, beyond even the mountains of the innocent slain at Belsen and Dachau to a fearful contemplation of the diabolical force behind the aberrations of the spirit which deform our so-called civilization. This is the ground on which Lewis chooses to give battle; the dragon of the Book of Revelation is again brought to bay.

The story of *That Hideous Strength* takes place in modern England; as Lewis says in the Preface, "vaguely 'after the [Second World] war.'" Mark Studdock, a young scholar who holds what might be called a Research Fellowship in Sociology at the small University of Edgestow, temporarily leaves his post to investigate a position with the N.I.C.E. (the National Institute of Co-ordinated Experiments), at Belbury. Gradually it begins to dawn on him that he is virtually a prisoner at the Institute, and the form of vast evil emerges. In effect the N.I.C.E. is an organization inspired and guided by transplanetary spirits of darkness, bent not only on destroying the good in humankind but even in creating a new kind of Man. To accomplish its ends the Institute employs the usual methods of totalitarianism: corruption of the press, wholesale and callous use of the lie as a political instrument, appropriation of "necessary" private property, and special police trained in all the refinements of violence. Against this monstrous perversion a counterforce comes into being. At the manor house of St. Anne's near Edgestow there collects almost by chance a small group of dedicated men and women. Their leader is a man known sometimes as Mr. Fisher-King, sometimes by his earthly name, Ransom. A onetime philologist at Cambridge University, he had voyaged to the planets Venus and Mars (as described in Lewis' novels *Perelandra* and *Out of the Silent Planet*) and had come face to face with the Powers of Light and Darkness. He is also the Pendragon of Britain, by virtue of his position committed to the establishment of the holy kingdom of Logres. In the company headed by Ransom, Studdock's wife Jane plays an important part, because of her unique ability to see in dreams the operations of the enemy at Belbury. As the conflict grows, both sides realize the importance of enlisting the help of the ancient Welsh seer Merlinus Ambrosius, who lies buried in a state of suspended animation under a wood near the University. In the nick of time Merlinus leaves his tomb of his own free will and joins forces with Ransom at St. Anne's. The story then moves swiftly to its conclusion. With the help of Merlinus, Belbury is utterly destroyed; the invaders who had established a virtual dictatorship over town and gown of Edgestow are swallowed up in a vast convulsion of nature, and Mark returns to Jane. The horrors of the N.I.C.E. had purged his mind of an earlier desire to be "important," and his heart is filled with new meaning for a marriage which up to then had been hollow for them both.

From this summary one can see that Lewis' novel is profoundly affected by catastrophes as yet unrealized when Williams wrote *War in Heaven*. As a tract for the times, therefore, it is much more specifically pointed than the earlier novel. The brutalities of what totalitarianism has been and what it might be in the future add great dramatic excitement to *That Hideous Strength*. This difference apart, however, the two books are very similar in basic assumptions. Both authors place the power of the Grail at the center of a universal conflict between good and evil, and both see the Arthurian legend as a constantly active means of conveying spiritual lessons for succeeding generations. Modern England as well as Joseph of Arimathea's Glastonbury is a proper habitation for the Grail. This attitude is diametrically opposed to Addison's smug dogmatism in regard to Spenser:

> the mystic tale, that pleased of yore,
> Can charm an understanding age no more.

In speaking of the Holy Grail, Williams makes a point which applies to the whole cycle: "It is not, as in Tennyson, only for the elect; it is for all."[53] So the Arthurian legend is for all men and all times. To Williams and Lewis as re-creators of spiritual Logres it is not sufficient merely to give the ancient stories the ethical or social coloring of one's day, as do Tennyson and indeed most writers whose versions are remembered. The moral and religious forces within Arthur's kingdom must be kept alive in tales of contemporary setting. The Grail is far more than a misty symbol of the far away and long ago.

This belief in the present power of the legend does not mean that traditional Arthurian material is submerged or attenuated in *That Hideous Strength*. It is true that of the familiar figures in the story only two appear: Merlin and the guardian of the Grail, Ransom.[54] Yet the whole novel embodies the moral and spiritual conflict of an ancient time. Early in the book, Dr. Dimble (later revealed as an important member of the "Company" at St. Anne's) talks to Jane Studdock about the Arthurian legend. He explains Arthur as "a man of the old British line, but also a Christian and a fully-trained general with Roman technique,[55] trying to pull this whole society together and almost succeeding." Dimble also tells of the tensions within Arthurian society: the jealousies among the Britons themselves, the superior attitude of the "Romanised section" (the Launcelots and Lionels), and, as an unexplained and yet powerful force, the "tug back to druidism." Here Merlin comes into the conversation, and in such a way as to lay the groundwork for interplanetary mythmaking:

"I often wonder," said Dr. Dimble, "whether Merlin doesn't represent the last trace of something the later tradition has quite forgotten about — something that became impossible when the only people in touch with the supernatural were either white or black, either priests or sorcerers."[56]

This is to say that Merlinus Ambrosius is far from being the usual enchanter, skilled in transformations and prophecies. In Lewis' novel he is a survival of immemorially old occult powers; he is the last inheritor of the Atlantean magic which lay behind the emergence into form of the essences within chaos. As such he is in touch with forces so ancient that he is a creature suspended in the infinity of time; coming to the present haltingly, effective as an instrument of vengeance, yet incapable of the strength which came to Ransom through the post-Atlantean power of the Holy Grail.

The warfare between Light and Darkness which makes *That Hideous Strength* so exciting is centered on Arthur's struggle (removed though he is) to build a spiritual kingdom. As in Williams, Arthur is the central agent in a long-continuing effort to transform Britain into Logres, a land to be freed from the assaults of evil spirits beyond the world which had long kept our planet under siege. Dr. Dimble explains the situation in historical terms:

It all began . . . when we discovered that the Arthurian story is mostly true history. There was a moment in the Sixth Century when something that is always trying to break through into this country nearly succeeded. Logres was our name for it — it will do as well as another. And then . . . gradually we began to see all English history in a new way. We discovered the haunting. . . . How something we may call Britain is always haunted by something we may call Logres. Haven't you noticed that we are two countries? After every Arthur, a Mordred; behind every Milton, a Cromwell; a nation of poets, a nation of shopkeepers; the home of Sidney — and of Cecil Rhodes. Is it any wonder they call us hypocrites? But what they mistake for hypocrisy is really the struggle between Logres and Britain.[57]

In the struggle which destroys the hideous strength of Belbury, Ransom, like Archdeacon Davenant of *War in Heaven*, is the instrument of victory. To readers accustomed to the tense physical danger, the cut and thrust of most Arthurian tales, his metaphysical serenity may be misleading. Actually he is a person of the greatest power. As Pendragon of Britain, dedicated, like Williams' Merlin, to the establishment of Arthur's holy kingdom of Logres, he is in direct touch with the agents of Light, and draws from them a serene confidence, a transparent goodness which, like the purity of the Lady in *Comus,* needs no other armor. This does not mean that Ransom is a disembodied spiritual symbol; in fact he is very much of a man.[58] His spiritual importance as the possessor of the holy secret is constantly tempered by the fact that he is also credible as a human being. With great skill, he wins the allegiance of the bewildered Celt, Merlinus Ambrosius, and he has wise words to say to Jane on the subject of marriage.[59] He is, in fact, a high union of body and spirit — flesh suffused with heavenly joy.

That Hideous Strength deserves an honored place in the Arthurian legend, for it is a highly original restatement of old truths applied to our violent, distraught world, and it is conceived in terms of vaulting imagination. It would be difficult to surpass the sheer excitement of this book. The shadow of a massive perversion of the human mind and spirit hovers over it. Belbury, like the octopods of P'o-l'u, spreads its tentacles: the very trees are to be replaced by substitutes in aluminum and the race of men by a scientific, disembodied monstrosity. Yet the Light of Heaven also shines, piercing the fogs above beleaguered Edgestow and striking the manor house of St. Anne's. There, as the moment approaches for the triumph of Arthur's Logres over the maleficence of Belbury, Ransom receives the gods of the other planets. Like Charles Williams, Lewis skillfully makes us feel rather than see supernatural visitations. Mystery, beauty, and danger beat upon the reader in pulsating suggestion; the air throbs with power. Ransom alone knows the features of the gods; his "Company" at St. Anne's can only wonder and believe.

The new intensity of wonder and belief have added great strength to the annals of Logres. Just as Henry Adams in America returned to the thirteenth century in rediscovering the power of the Virgin as against the modern power of the Dynamo, so Arthurians of the twentieth century have believed that they should reaffirm the religious significance of the legend. Not that the story of the Grail has ever lacked it, at least in a conventional sense, save in the works of certain modern skeptics. Setting aside the question of its remote origins, the legend as recorded has been almost invariably Christian. Yet after the Middle Ages it has not had the immediacy which Charles Williams and C. S. Lewis give it. Especially it has not often had their acute sense of the theological meaning of the Cup as a symbol of present power, and not simply as something precious to be found. Since the time of Malory few authors have sensed the unique power of the Grail. Tennyson does so only fleetingly in *The Holy Grail*. He comes closer to succeeding in "Sir Galahad," a poem which deserves to be remembered for its attempt to describe some of the mystery of the Grail rather than for a hero whose "strength is as the strength of ten because [his] heart is pure." R. S. Hawker's *The Quest of the Sangraal* (1864) has one or two interesting passages suggesting the modern attitude, especially his mention of the "Great Cone of Space" and the "Numynous Light" of the eastern sky which stretches over Galahad. Even in the very word "Cone," Hawker hints at the splendor Williams was later to give his cosmology.

None of the forerunners, however, brought all the elements together so successfully as the later devotees — the grandeur of the universe, the gigantic warfare between good and evil, the power resting in the Grail itself, and the undemanding serenity of the Grail-Champion. Never before had the spiritual implications of the Arthurian legend been so fully realized.

Once again the old stories have been written for our learning, so that in a new Waste Land never imagined by the Fisher-King we may see the stupendous vision both of evil and of ineffable grace, and seeing it may find a highway through the desert.

Notes

CHAPTER ONE

1. *The Life of Sir Aglovale de Galis* (1905), p. 264.
2. *Ibid.*
3. *Songs and Satires* (1916), p. 141.
4. *Ibid.*, p. 154.
5. *Gwenevere* (1905), pp. 25, 29.
6. *Ibid.*, p. 13.
7. *Ibid.*, p. 18.
8. It is this conflict between the romanticism implicit in the old stories both in substance and mood and the realism so prevalent in twentieth-century literature which helps to explain some of the most interesting versions later in the century. Generally speaking, realism comes to be more and more important, especially, as with Robinson, in reinterpreting the stories with the help of modern psychology. Yet the romantic elements persist, in the re-creation of a lost world, and in the emphasis on passionate feeling.
9. *Enid* (1908), p. 24.
10. Many more Arthurian poems of this sort were written in the twentieth century than before, and by poets of standing such as Robert P. Tristram Coffin, Gustav Davidson, Edna St. Vincent Millay, and Sara Teasdale. See Northup and Parry's Bibliography for a comprehensive listing.
11. "The Great Return," in *The Caerleon Edition of the Works of Arthur Machen* (1923), Vol. 7, p. 230.
12. His originality was startling to some readers. See Machen's amusing account of the reviewer in the *Times Literary Supplement* (London)

who stated that "it was nonsense to be romancing about the Grail at all, since it had been proved to be merely a Feeding Vessel of pagan-Irish origin. . . . He protested against the Grail being manifested, as in my story, to quite common people, such as farmers and grocers. And I admit that it *was* low. But the Order of the British Empire was not in existence when the book was written. If it ever goes into a new edition – which seems unlikely – I shall certainly make all the characters O. B. E.'s." See Henry Danielson, *Arthur Machen: A Bibliography* (1923), p. 45.

13. See particularly *The Secret Glory, infra,* Chap. VII.

14. There is a strong suggestion of the cosmic struggle between good and evil in Machen's short story "Guinevere and Lancelot," published (with Arthurian essays) in *T. P.'s Weekly,* 1908–1909. At one point, in a completely new addition to the story, Guinevere visits a sorcerer, who calls up the devils of hell to ensure her success with Lancelot: "[There was] a noise and a rushing sound amongst the black branches and thickets of the wood, the great boughs of the trees tossed one on another, and said the wizard: 'Now, madam, the Hosts of the Air draw near; now is at hand the army of Tzabaoth.' Then, in the shimmering and in the shining of the glassy smoke there showed the shapes of the Mighty Ones, and to the Mightiest did Guinevere there make offering of herself."

15. *Guinevere* (1906), p. 41.

16. T. Sturge Moore has said of this poem "How felicitously the language rises to gnomic force without losing naturalness!" ("The Legend of Tristram and Isolt in Modern Poetry," *Criterion,* I [Oct. 1922], 45.)

17. "The Death of Tristram," in *Odes* (1901), p. 39.

18. Two other versions of the Tristram story, though inferior to Binyon's, show something of his strong feeling: *The Tragedy of Pardon* (1911) and "Tristan de Léonois" in *The Accuser* (1911), both plays written by Michael Field (Katherine Harris Bradley and Edith Emma Cooper). The second of these is better than the first, and makes use of some rather out-of-the-way material, for instance, the meeting between the lovers after Tristan's madness, when he comes to Mark's court disguised as a fool – a scene possibly suggested by the Old French *La Folie Tristan* (Oxford version). Here, and in other scenes, especially Iseult's stormy trip to Brittany, we find somewhat modern use of emotion, even bordering on the pathological.

19. *Tristram and Isoult* (1913), p. 6.

20. *Ibid.,* p. 61.

21. *Ibid.,* pp. 83, 87.

22. The stories of Arthur have been kept before a wide audience by their popularity with children. During the first part of this century a great many tales of this sort were published, most of them adaptations of Malory. Of these the best are the Arthurian stories in Andrew Lang's *Book of Romance* (1902), and Howard Pyle's series: *The Story of King*

Arthur and His Knights (1903), *The Story of the Champions of the Round Table* (1905), *The Story of Sir Launcelot and His Companions* (1907), and *The Story of the Grail and the Passing of Arthur* (1910).

CHAPTER TWO

1. The works of Charles Williams, which occupy a large part of the final chapter, while they also reflect the chaos of our day, are far more dependent on ancient truth than on present discontents. And in giving his cycle a profoundly spiritual and theological basis Williams is poles apart from any of the authors included above.

2. The most useful full-length biography at present is by Hermann Hagedorn (1938). There are many commentaries on him. Among the most helpful are Charles Cestre's *An Introduction to Edwin Arlington Robinson* (1930), Yvor Winters' *Edwin Arlington Robinson* (1946), Emery Neff's *Edwin Arlington Robinson* (1948), and Ellsworth Barnard's *Edwin Arlington Robinson* (1952).

3. Hermann Hagedorn, *Edwin Arlington Robinson* (1938), pp. 38, 162, 200.

4. For further evidence on this point and an interesting summary of contemporary judgments on Robinson's Arthurian poems see Richard Crowder, "E. A. Robinson's Camelot," *College English*, IX (1947) 72–79.

5. Yvor Winters, p. 146, speaks to this point when he states that Robinson, far from being the standard-bearer of a new tradition, is the last of an old one — that of certain masters of American prose: Henry James, Edith Wharton, Motley, and Parkman. The affinity of Robinson's reflective and analytical method of characterization with that of the first two authors will be sufficiently evident. It might be added, however, that while in general Winters' argument against Robinson's innovation holds, it does not do so in regard to Arthurian story. Here his originality is strikingly evident.

6. *Merlin,* in *Collected Poems* (1922), pp. 241–242.

7. *Ibid.,* p. 249.

8. *Ibid.,* p. 263.

9. It is impossible not to see in Robinson's crumbling world of Camelot his own world, shaken by the First World War. This penetration of the old world by present disaster adds all the more somber force to the poem.

10. *Merlin,* in *Collected Poems* (1922), p. 257..

11. Nor does Modred appear in Robinson's *Lancelot* (1920). Though Robinson wrote quite a long passage describing the plotting of Modred, Colgrevance, and Agravaine against Lancelot and Guinevere he did not include it in the published *Lancelot*. It was brought out separately in

a limited edition as *Modred: A Fragment* (The Brick Row Bookshop of New York, 1929).

12. *Merlin,* in *Collected Poems* (1922), p. 314.

13. *Ibid.,* p. 306.

14. Hagedorn, p. 320.

15. Winters, p. 85.

16. *Lancelot,* in *Collected Poems* (1922), p. 421.

17. Described in Robinson's *Modred. Vide supra,* n. 11.

18. Mark Van Doren, *Edwin Arlington Robinson* (1927), p. 72.

19. *Lancelot,* in *Collected Poems* (1922), p. 389.

20. *Ibid.,* pp. 445–446.

21. It is a little difficult to understand Amy Lowell's point of view toward this conclusion. "The only hint of poignance in the end of the poem is the very failure of the 'Light' to emit any warm glow. Lancelot riding away, seeking to comfort himself by this wan flame, is a pathetic figure." ("A Bird's-Eye View of E. A. Robinson," *The Dial* [Feb. 1922], p. 141.)

22. It consists of twenty-two poems dealing with Arthurian situations, from the King's birth to the last battle with Modred. For the most part the poems are detached episodes or sketches rather than connected narrative.

23. *Camelot* (1919), p. 12.

24. The picture of Lancelot given here, as in John Erskine's *Galahad* (1926) (*vide infra,* pp. 43–45), is not in keeping with "the tendency [since about 1850] to render Lancelot faultless and to ennoble him at any cost." (August J. App, *Lancelot in English Literature* [1929], p. 215.)

25. The late John Erskine, who was Professor of English Literature at Columbia University, wrote other modern interpretations of Arthurian stories, particularly *Tristan and Isolde* (1932).

26. *Galahad,* p. 16.

27. *Ibid.,* p. 194.

28. *Ibid.,* p. 26.

29. The modern approach to the "Tragedy of Camelot," and something of Erskine's manner are also seen in James Bridie's play "Lancelot," published in *Plays for Plain People* (1944). Merlin appears at the beginning with the serious purpose of finding the perfect man as the expression of the age of chivalry which he has created. In the main the plot follows a sober course. Yet Bridie cannot resist incongruously waggish details, such as saying, when Lancelot is deceived into bedding with Elaine, that "Dame Brisen hocussed his drink." A number of times also the dialogue is self-consciously "smart" and aphoristic, and some of the wit — especially Arthur's attempt to convince Pelleas that Guenevere must die by fire — is secondhand Shaw.

30. *The Ill-Made Knight* (1940), p. 174.

31. *Ibid.,* p. 284.

CHAPTER THREE

1. A recent version, Ruth Collier Sharpe's novel, *Tristram of Lyonesse* (1949), is less traditional than old-fashioned. The passion of the lovers is largely submerged in a welter of adventures which sometimes take Tristram very far from home, and the whole is written in a highly decorated prose. The ending — a happy one — completely changes the story, for the worse.

2. Note the remarks made about Iseult in Symons' "Iseult of Brittany" (published in *Cesare Borgia*, 1920), a brief, simple play touched with elegiac sadness for the fate of Tristan's wife in France. Iseult of Brittany says of her rival:

> *She has a mind*
> *More manly-hearted than a man's.*

And Ygraine, a lady-in-waiting of Duke Jovelin's Breton entourage, calls Iseult of Ireland cruel by nature:

> *As a noble beast;*
> *Not crafty, not for less than hate or death.*

3. *Tristan and Iseult* (1917), pp. 48-51.

4. *Ibid.*, p. 106.

5. Cf. Erhard Heimann, *Tristan und Isolde in der neuzeitlichen Literatur* (1930), p. 78: "überall ist Tristan [in Symons' play] der passive Teil. Iseult dagegen kennt keine Gewissensfragen; ihr geht die Liebe über alles."

6. *Tristan and Iseult*, pp. 48, 73.

7. Symons increases the irony of the situation and the psychological conflict of the women by making the two Iseults cousins.

8. *Tristan and Iseult*, p. 90.

9. Cf. Maurice Halperin, *Le Roman de Tristan et Iseut dans la Littérature Anglo-Américaine au XIXᵉ et au XXᵉ Siècles* (1931), pp. 95–96: "Le génie poétique de Symons consiste à donner au lecteur une impression d'une simplicité d'expression presque trop sévère accompagnée de toute la profondeur de la passion la plus intime de l'âme humaine." Perhaps Halperin overstates the case when he goes on to say "Inutile de remarquer que sans ce souffle de génie lyrique, ses vers . . . restent impuissants."

10. *Isolt of Ireland* (1927), p. 61.

11. *Ibid.*, p. 41.

12. *The Famous Tragedy of the Queen of Cornwall* (1923), p. 17.

13. *In the Mill* (1941), pp. 44–48.

14. Note his reconstruction of the "historical" Arthur in *Badon Parchments* (1947), described in Chapter IV.

15. With the kind permission of Mr. Masefield, I reproduce in this paragraph material received through conversation and correspondence.

16. J. D. Bruce summarizes the evidence concerning Pictish origin in *The Evolution of Arthurian Romance* (1923), I, pp. 178–180. An Irish chronicle of the eighth-century Picts mentions "Drest [which gives in turn Drostan and Tristan] filius Talorcan." Fragments of the tale as carried over from the Picts to the Welsh may be found in the *Mabinogion* and the *Triads*. See particularly the latter (*Les Mabinogion,* ed. J. Loth [1913], II, pp. 270–272), for an account of Drystan's guarding the swine of March (i.e., Mark), son of Meirchyon.

17. It should be noted that Arthur is not really one of the conspirators. He takes part in the pig-stealing unenthusiastically, apparently more as a practical joke than anything else, and elsewhere refuses to join in plotting.

18. Halperin, p. 131, refers to "Le parfum de la porcherie qui ne quitte jamais *Tristan and Isolt.*"

19. Notice that in a complete departure from tradition, Tristan dies a natural death; particularly that he is not slain by Marc, or with his connivance. His death follows a terrible and climactic falling out with Isolt and is not, as in many of the versions, the result of more or less casual and momentary brutality. Yet though Masefield leaves tradition in describing Tristan's death, he returns to it movingly in one detail. The dying lover sings a touching lyric, ending "Isolt my blood, Isolt my breath, / In you my life; in you my death" — clearly modeled after Thomas' well-known lines: "Isot ma drue, Isot m'amie, / en vos ma mort, en vos ma vie." The manner of Tristan's end helps to keep Marc from being a degraded character. Though he is not too clear in Masefield's play he is more credible than some authors have made him.

20. *Tristan and Isolt* (1927), pp. 126–127.

21. *Ibid.,* p. 133. Arthur's speech, however, does not close the play. There follows a brief Epilogue, in which Destiny says that things happen "not as men plan, nor as women pray" but rather as shaped by the spirit of man and the judgment of God in bringing our pride to the dust. After the vigor of the final catastrophe and Arthur's moving speech of catharsis this Epilogue seems redundant.

22. Masefield's interest in the story and his originality of imaginative creation are further shown in two poems appearing in *Minnie Maylow's Story* (1931). "The Love Gift" introduces a magnanimous Marc, who receives the gift of immortality to be bestowed upon another. He gives it to Isolt, as of doubtful benefit; she passes it to Brangwen, who finally returns it to Marc. Somewhat cast down, he presents it to a boy whose mother is dying. "Tristan's Singing" is a poem of fresh, lyrical feeling. It concerns a joyous midsummer song the mad Tristan composed at the bidding of Nature. Though he is cast out by Marc when he attempts to sing the song before him, he lifts his voice in the forest and is joined by Isolt. Before the eyes of Dinan's son they are transfigured; they lose their rags and robes to take wings. "Shining like stars and flying like the plover / Laughing aloft and singing away / Into some Summer knowing

no decay." Here madness, love, and death are all touched with trans-figuration. The poem successfully suggests the sweep and passion of the legend.

23. Unlike Malory, Mrs. Closs does not make Tristan a contemporary (and even associate) of Arthur and his knights. In her novel Tristan and Iseult of Brittany, for example, read in a book of Lancelot and Guinevere, and of other knights of the Round Table (pp. 291, 293).

24. *Tristan*, p. xi.

25. *Ibid.*, p. 153.

26. Jan. 18, 1941. The reviewer also objects to the sentimentality and the romanticized style of the novel. In this connection see also a letter written to the same journal (Feb. 8, 1941) by Dorothy K. Coveney of the University of Wales, taking exception to the reviewer's remarks.

27. A vastly more allusive and influential novel than Mrs. Closs's may be mentioned very briefly. There are references to the Tristram story in James Joyce's *Finnegans Wake* (1943), in which Isobel Earwicker is possibly meant to be identified with Isolt, but the allusions are so fleeting and cryptic that Joyce's novel is of scant interest in the history of the legend.

28. As yet there is no clear-cut agreement as to the permanent place of Robinson's *Tristram*. See the divergent views of various critics (Harriet Monroe, William Rose Benét, Edmund Wilson, and others) in "E. A. Robinson's Camelot," by Richard Crowder, *College English*, IX, 1947, 72–79. Judgments pro and con may be found in Charles Cestre's *An Introduction to Edwin Arlington Robinson* (1930) and Yvor Winters' *Edwin Arlington Robinson* (1946). Mark Van Doren, in his brief book, *Edwin Arlington Robinson*, published in the same year as *Tristram*, calls it "the best [version] in English since the Middle Ages."

29. Hermann Hagedorn, *Edwin Arlington Robinson* (1938), pp. 162, 200.

30. *Ibid.*, p. 310.

31. *Ibid.*, p. 340.

32. Earlier writers, of course, had sometimes condensed the Tristram story or used only excerpts from it. See, for example, the thirteenth-century *La Folie Tristan*, Tennyson's "The Last Tournament," and Matthew Arnold's "Tristram and Iseult." In general, however, contemporary writers have tended to abbreviate the narrative more often than previously.

33. As quoted in Hagedorn, p. 341.

34. *Tristram*, p. 70.

35. *Ibid.*, p. 45.

36. *Ibid.*, pp. 22–23.

37. Louise Dauner, for example, says that Robinson sees all women as "disturbing, provocative, and both the harbingers and agents of tragedy." ("The Pernicious Rib: E. A. Robinson's Concept of Feminine Character," *American Literature*, XV [1943], 147.)

38. *Tristram,* p. 160.
39. *Ibid.,* p. 193.
40. *Ibid.,* p. 172.
41. *Edwin Arlington Robinson,* p. 224.
42. *Tristram,* pp. 97–98.
43. This remark may stand even in spite of Robinson's insistence that *Tristram* represents what is for him a new approach to passion. In a letter to Mrs. Louis Ledoux (Aug. 3, 1925) he says: "The key and color of the thing are altogether different from those of *Merlin* and *Lancelot,* and may cause some readers to suspect that I'm getting a little tired of hearing too much about my New England reticence — which may be pretty true." (Quoted in Neff, p. 222.)
44. It is hard to agree with Charles Cestre (p. 102) when he says that in *Tristram* Robinson "eschews the pitfall of too much analysis."
45. *The Idea of a Theater* (Doubleday Anchor reprint of 1953), p. 89.
46. Denham Sutcliffe (ed.), *Untriangulated Stars* (1947), p. 247.
47. *Tristram,* p. 206.

CHAPTER FOUR

1. The point made by Nennius that Arthur helped the kings of the Britons in war (not being a king himself) is explained by R. G. Collingwood and J. N. L. Myres in *Roman Britain and the English Settlements* (1936), p. 321: "To say that [Arthur] fought 'with the kings of the Britons' implies that his commission was valid all over the country, and that he fought not in any one kingdom or region, but wherever he was wanted, co-operating with the local levies. His was, in fact, a mobile field-army." This is clearly the view taken by both Edward Frankland and John Masefield. Not only on this point but also on the whole question of the historical Arthur and what he probably did, Collingwood and Myres are admirably clear.
2. See also his *Heroes of Chivalry and Romance* (1896), which includes "King Arthur and The Round Table."
3. Similar to Church's story in general method are W. H. Babcock's *Cian of the Chariots* [*ca.* 1898] and C. M. Case's *The Banner of the White Horse* (1916).
4. One other, *Love Among the Ruins* (1904), is vaguely set in the Middle Ages. Modred and Tristram are mentioned as knights of Flavian of Gambrevault, Lord of Avalon, and there are a few other Arthurian allusions. It is not, however, an Arthurian story.
5. *Uther and Igraine* (new ed., 1928), p. 130.
6. This statement appears in an account of British history given by Hallard to Aurelius Superbus, *The Man Who Went Back* (1940), p. 181.
7. *Ibid.,* p. 87.
8. *The Altar of the Legion* (1926), p. 278.

9. Arthur Conan Doyle's short story, "The Last of the Legions," in *The Last Galley* (1911), also deals with Roman Britain near the time of Arthur, though in this case before his day and not after. The story tells of the withdrawal of the Roman legions from Britain for the defence of Rome, and the resultant anxiety of the Britons. There is nothing specifically Arthurian in Doyle's tale, save for the mention of Mordred as the "wild chief of the western Cymri."

10. *A History of the Anglo-Saxons* (1935), I, p. 37.

11. Probably this Guitolin was suggested by the Guitolinus of the *Annales Cambriae,* who is mentioned as struggling with Ambrosius ("discordiam Guitolini et Ambrosii"). See *Les Mabinogion,* ed. J. Loth (1913), II, p. 371. (The text of the *Annales Cambriae* is on pp. 370–382 of Vol. II of this edition.)

12. The story purports to be told to Beli ap Rhun by his grandfather Artorius, shortly before the latter's death in the year 540. Beli, who became King of Gwynedd, wrote the story from memory some years later in the monastery of Bangor.

13. *Pendragon* (1930), p. 3.

14. *Ibid.*

15. A crude, primitive form of the Round Table appears in the circular trench dug for the Gorsedd (Council) at the feast of Beltane. In this trench (about two feet deep and provided with seats) sat the members of the Council, facing each other over a space of level turf, in the center of which was piled wood for a fire. As Faraday says, "Such a circle we in Britain call a Gorsedd, and it sets forth the equality of all men, be they princes or kerns, before the law of Britain; for there is neither beginning nor end to the circle, neither first place nor last place." (*Pendragon,* p. 229.) Cf. the accounts of primitive Celtic tables in A. C. L. Brown, "The Round Table before Wace," [Harvard] *Studies and Notes in Philology and Literature,* VII (1900).

16. One is reminded of his importance in the romances as an agent in establishing Arthur on the throne when he wishes to make Artorius the "Pendragon" of Britain, i.e., the traditional overlord. Artorius declines his help saying "I am also a Roman, and place small value upon this title of Pendragon." (*Pendragon,* p. 230.)

17. It is worth mentioning that Faraday, a barrister by profession, is a Fellow of the Royal Historical Society, and that in the Introduction to *Pendragon* he presents his novel as "the true story of the life of Arthur, as far as I can gather it from many scattered sources."

18. For much of the material in this paragraph I am indebted to Mr. Frankland himself, who has kindly given me permission to use statements made in conversation and correspondence.

19. In line with the concept of Arthur as a war-leader rather than a prince, notice Arthur's disclaimer to his troops after his accession to power. He claims to be no "Guletic," but a simple soldier who will lead them in war. (*The Bear of Britain* [1944], p. 42.)

20. In the Afterword to *The Bear of Britain* the author acknowledges his indebtedness to Nennius, Gildas, the *Annales Cambriae,* and Welsh poetry.

21. *The Bear of Britain,* p. 90. There is a faint suggestion later that the Round Table may have chivalric and even religious significance. Arthur finds the hermit Carannog's round wooden altar table after it has drifted to the seashore and gives orders to have it taken to Camelot, saying that perhaps it will be like the earlier turf one. "A sign it may be that our fellowship shall endure and yet prove fruitful" (p. 184).

22. For a brief discussion of theories concerning the knotty question of Arthur's name, and especially its relationship to the Celtic word for "bear," see J. D. Bruce, *The Evolution of Arthurian Romance* (1923), I, pp. 4–5, n.4. See also E. K. Chambers, *Arthur of Britain* (1927), *passim,* and W. A. Nitze, "Arthurian Names: Arthur," *PMLA,* LXIV (1949), 585–596, 1235.

23. It is worth remembering that in the lives of certain British Saints composed in the eleventh and twelfth centuries Arthur's reputation was not good. Arthur G. Brodeur, one of the coauthors of *The Altar of the Legion,* already discussed, states in his article "Arthur, Dux Bellorum," in *University of California Publications in English,* III, No. 7 (1939), that the reason for this unpopularity with the church may have been ruthless usurpation on his part. "His death may have been caused by the revolt of a displaced prince of the legitimate line" (p. 263). And he continues by calling attention to the death of Arthur and Medraut together in the *Annales Cambriae.*

24. *The Bear of Britain,* p. 86.

25. *Ibid.,* p. 203. The vast moral conflict here suggested reflects an ancient Welsh tradition. See A. C. L. Brown, "Arthur's Loss of Queen and Kingdom," *Speculum,* XV (1940), 11: "The hypothesis that we must adopt evidently is that Arthur's last battle at Camlan was regarded by the ancient Welsh as an Armageddon or ultimate conflict between good and evil. Arthur's opponent was regarded as evil personified, as the old dragon, or as the principle of evil or death. Long before Geoffrey's time, we must suppose that oral traditions had identified the usurper with death."

26. *In the Mill* (1941), pp. 113–114.

27. *Badon Parchments* (1947), p. 4.

28. *Ibid.,* p. 150.

29. *Ibid.,* p. 52.

30. *Ibid.,* p. 61.

31. *Ibid.,* p. 52.

32. *Ibid.,* p. 25.

33. *The Bear of Britain* and *Badon Parchments* (especially the latter) emphasize Arthur's use of cavalry. Doubtless both Mr. Masefield and Frankland were familiar with the extremely interesting and convincing point made by Collingwood and Myres (pp. 322–324) to the effect

that in all likelihood Arthur, trained in the Imperial army, introduced cavalry — lately established in the Roman forces — in British campaigning. The association of Arthur with mounted knights in the romances makes this theory all the more likely. "The knight of the middle ages was in fact only a survival or revival of the late Roman *eques cataphractarius*" (p. 324). See also Duggan's *Conscience of the King* (1951).

34. *Badon Parchments,* p. 47.
35. *Ibid.,* p. 63.
36. *Ibid.,* pp. 111–112.
37. One other recent novel may be briefly noticed. John Cowper Powys' *Porius* (1951) is a long and ambitious attempt to describe, apparently in terms of political allegory, eight days in October, A.D. 499, when King Arthur, Amherawdr (i.e. Emperor) of Britain, tries to unite diverse factions in north Wales against the Anglo-Saxon invaders. Though the novel shows Powys' enormous romantic love of early Welsh legend and scene, it is not a successful account of great events on the march just before the battle of Badon Hill. Arthur does not often appear in the story, and the action (relatively little) has the fragmentary, static quality of dream. Other Arthurian characters include Myrddin (Merlin), a sage of vast philosophical and vaticinative power, his nemesis Nineue, Arthur's nephew Medrawd, and even Galahault (Galahad), Prince of Surluse. But the cast is so large and so allusively introduced, and the fortunes of Porius in trying to help Arthur are so elliptically told that apart from memorable scenes of description the total effect is bewildering.

CHAPTER FIVE

1. An exception is Floyd Dell's one-act play, *King Arthur's Socks* (1922), which takes place in Camelot, Maine, and describes the triangular love-dalliance of Professor Arthur B. Robinson, his wife Guenevere, and their friend Vivien(!).
2. Published respectively in *Sonnets to a Red-Haired Lady and Famous Love Affairs* (1922) and *Sir Galahad and Other Rimes* (1936).
3. *Gawayne and the Green Knight* (1904), p. 31.
4. *Jurgen* (15th printing, 1924), p. 109.
5. *The Sword in the Stone* (New York, 1939), pp. 32–33.
6. *Ibid.,* p. 83.
7. *Ibid.,* p. 210.
8. The giant Galapas whom Arthur slays in Bk. V of the *Morte Darthur* (first cutting him down to size by striking off his legs at the knees) may very well have been Italian also, for he fought in the Emperor Lucius' Roman army.
9. *The Sword in the Stone* (New York, 1939), p. 268.
10. *Ibid.,* pp. 305–306.
11. *The Witch in the Wood* (1939), p. 23.

12. *Ibid.*, p. 111.
13. *Ibid.*, pp. 111–112.
14. *Ibid.*, pp. 217–220.
15. *Ibid.*, p. 19.
16. This scene contains a hint of sinister events that were to flame later in the "Orkney feud." Agravaine, in a hysterical fit of jealousy, associates Meg the kitchenmaid (the virgin who lures the unicorn) with his mother, and dispatches the animal because it puts its head in his "mother's" lap. It is worth noting also that the four boys are not at all pleased at their mother's flirtatious ways with Grummore and Pellinore, especially the latter, whose important part in the feud is well-known.

CHAPTER SIX

1. See J. D. Bruce's *The Evolution of Arthurian Romance* (1923), I, p. 143, and the introductory commentary to J. J. Parry's edition of the *Vita Merlini* (1925).
2. "Merlin's Grave," pp. 69–70.
3. *Ibid.*, p. 76.
4. *The Madness of Merlin* (1947), pp. viii–ix.
5. *Ibid.*, p. 11.
6. *Ibid.*, p. 45.
7. *Ibid.*, p. 8.
8. *Ibid.*, p. 28.
9. *Descent into Hell* (1937), p. 172.
10. *That Hideous Strength* (reprint of Oct. 1946), p. 24.

CHAPTER SEVEN

1. Other scholars, however, have emphasized the Christian nature of the story; for example, Lizette A. Fisher, *The Mystic Vision in the* Grail *Legend and in The Divine Comedy* (1917); Rose J. Peebles, *The Legend of Longinus in Ecclesiastical Tradition and in English Literature* (1911); J. D. Bruce, *The Evolution of Arthurian Romance* (1923), I, Part II, Chap. 1; and William J. Roach, "The Eucharistic Tradition in the *Perlesvaus*" (1939). Apart from the retellings here discussed this theory has also found expression in a popular novel by Thomas B. Costain: *The Silver Chalice* (1952), a story of the beautifully worked chalice for the protection of the Cup of the Last Supper made by command of Joseph of Arimathea.
2. T. S. Eliot acknowledges the pervasive influence of Miss Weston's book in his treatment of the Grail myth in *The Waste Land* (1922). Without reference to a full commentary, however, the reader will find it difficult to discover the elements of the legend, because of the inwardness and the involution of the symbolic approach. The Waste Land

of the maimed Fisher-King is the central motif, though for the most part it is treated in scenes of modern degeneration. Part V ("What the Thunder Said") deals with the journey of the Grail-Champion (not named or described) to the Chapel Perilous. Evidently he asks the needful questions, for lightning flashes and healing rain pours down. It may be noted in passing that the poem also includes reminiscences of Wagner's *Tristan und Isolde*.

3. See also Loomis' *Arthurian Tradition and Chrétien de Troyes* (1949).

4. *Autobiography* (1934), p. 82.

5. *A Glastonbury Romance* (1933), p. 140.

6. *Ibid.*, pp. 771–772.

7. *Ibid.*, p. 818. Cf. Powys' association of the Fisher-King's ritual with sex, in his novel, *Porius* (1951), pp. 103, 449.

8. *Maiden Castle* (1936), p. 260.

9. *Ibid.*, p. 266.

10. *Vide supra*, Chap. 1.

11. *Notes and Queries* (1926), pp. 59–66. The essays in this volume originally appeared in *T. P.'s Weekly*, 1908–1909.

12. *Ibid.*, p. 71.

13. First published in 1909, it was reissued in a revised and expanded form in 1933 as *The Holy Grail: Its Legends and Symbolism*.

14. See ll. 3332–3336:

> *Les seintes paroles dist t'a*
> *Ki sunt douces et precïeuses*
> *Et gracïeuses et pitieuses,*
> *Ki sunt proprement apelees*
> *Secrez dou Graal et nummees.*

(*Le Roman de L'Estoire dou Graal*, ed. W. A. Nitze, 1927).

15. *The Holy Grail*, p. 472.

16. *Ibid.*, p. 507.

17. *Ibid.*, p. 46.

18. *Ibid.*, p. 229.

19. *Ibid.*, p. 502.

20. *Ibid.*, p. 528.

21. *Ibid.*, p. 439.

22. Waite's attitude toward the Grail is closely followed by Francis Rolt-Wheeler in *Mystic Gleams from the Holy Grail*, London, 1948.

23. *Notes and Queries*, pp. 61, 62.

24. *The Glorious Mystery* (1924), pp. 2, 3.

25. *Ibid.*, p. 56.

26. *The Secret Glory* (1922), pp. 99–100.

27. Machen's emphasis on the Celtic aspect of the legend was the only major point of controversy between himself and Waite. The latter objects (*The Holy Grail*, p. 348, n. 1) to Machen's assumption that the

Grail worship was preserved in the ancient Celtic rather than the Roman Church.

28. His ability as a student of literature, even though he was largely self-schooled, received official recognition when Oxford granted him an honorary M.A., and when he was appointed Lecturer at the University during World War II.

29. *War in Heaven* (new edition, 1947), p. 144.

30. *Ibid.*, p. 140. The pulsating energy here described in the Cup probably was suggested by a line from Tennyson's *The Holy Grail* which Williams admired: "Rose-red with beatings in it, as if alive."

31. *Ibid.*, pp. 241, 244–245.

32. *Ibid.*, p. 42.

33. T. S. Eliot, "The Significance of Charles Williams" (radio broadcast delivered in England during 1946), *The Listener,* BBC (London, Dec. 19, 1946), p. 894.

34. *Three Plays* (1931), p. 2.

35. In a review of *Arthurian Torso* (1948), in *Time and Tide,* (Jan. 1, 1949), p. 14.

36. *Essays Presented to Charles Williams* (1947), Preface, p. xi.

37. In much that follows by way of explaining the poems, I am greatly indebted to C. S. Lewis' brilliant commentary in *Arthurian Torso.* This book includes Williams' unfinished prose history of the legend, "The Figure of Arthur," as well as Lewis' exegesis.

38. Here Williams is almost certainly remembering a passage in Lady Guest's "Taliessin," an English version of what is probably a sixteenth-century compilation of Welsh poetry and prose included in the *Mabinogion* (1849), III. Taliessin says "My original country is the region of the summer stars" (p. 373). Furthermore, the ranging imagination of Taliessin's songs in Lady Guest's version and their emphasis on Christian responsibility in the warfare between good and evil strongly suggest Williams' attitude.

39. The chief changes in detail are the elevation of the seer Taliessin to a place of central importance in the story, and the treatment of Nimue, whose nature and function are vastly different from anything we have seen before. Williams' Merlin is also very different from Malory's magician and counselor. He is mostly conceived in Robert de Borron's terms, as a supernatural figure whose purpose it is to bring the power of the Grail to Arthur's court. See Williams' discussion of Merlin in "The Figure of Arthur," *Arthurian Torso,* pp. 33–39.

40. *The Region of the Summer Stars* (1944), pp. 8–9.

41. *Ibid.*, p. 9.

42. *Ibid.*, pp. 16–17.

43. Note Williams' statement in "The Figure of Arthur" (*Arthurian Torso,* p. 83): "Vessels of plenty have nothing to do with it; were it true (as it is not) that the Grail had developed from them, it would

still have developed out of all common measurement. It is the central matter of the Matter of Britain."

44. *The Region of the Summer Stars,* p. 44.

45. See C. S. Lewis' explanation of the doctrine of Co-inherence in *Arthurian Torso,* particularly pp. 142–143 and 151.

46. *Taliessin Through Logres* (1938), p. 81.

47. Williams probably uses this spelling of the name to distinguish the mother of Galahad from Elayne, the wife of Bors.

48. *Taliessin Through Logres,* pp. 57–59.

49. *Ibid.,* pp. 85–88.

50. *The Death of Arthur* (1936), p. 9.

51. *Ibid.,* pp. 42–43.

52. *Mephistopheles and the Golden Apples* (1943), p. 57.

53. "The Figure of Arthur," *Arthurian Torso,* p. 84.

54. Arthur, as Ransom says, "sits in the House of Kings in the cup-shaped land of Abhalljin, beyond the seas of Lur in Perelandra." (*That Hideous Strength* [reprint of Oct. 1946], p. 322.)

55.. For reference to Arthur as the *dux bellorum* see Merlin's recollection of the battle of Badon Hill, during the descent of Mars to St. Anne's, *ibid.,* pp. 384–385.

56. *Ibid.,* p. 24.

57. *Ibid.,* pp. 441–442.

58. Mr. Lewis has informed that though he did not even realize it at the time, there is much of Charles Williams himself in his picture of Ransom.

59. There is a clear intimation in *That Hideous Strength* (p. 327) that Mark and Jane may represent Launcelot and Elaine, and that their child (yet to be born) may be the next Pendragon.

Bibliography

I

WORKS OF REFERENCE

ARTHURIAN STUDIES have flourished in the twentieth century. A comprehensive though confusingly arranged bibliography of the early legend will be found in J. D. Bruce's *The Evolution of Arthurian Romance from the Beginnings down to the Year 1300*, Göttingen: Vandenhoeck and Ruprecht; Baltimore: The Johns Hopkins Press, 2 vols., 1923. An indispensable guide to contemporary scholarship in the field is the continuing *Bibliography of Critical Arthurian Literature*, edited by John J. Parry. Two volumes, covering the years 1922–1929 and 1930–1935 were issued by the Modern Language Association of America in 1931 and 1936. In 1940 publication of the series was taken over by the *Modern Language Quarterly*, the June issue of which included a bibliography covering the years 1936–1939. (For this period Professor Parry was assisted by Professor Margaret Schlauch.) Since then the bibliography has appeared annually in *MLQ*. In 1949 the International Arthurian Society published its first *Bibliographical Bulletin*, listing current learned works, mostly on the legend prior to the sixteenth century. Also useful is the check list of Arthurian books in the Newberry Library, Chicago, compiled by Jane D. Harding, 1933 (with Supplement, 1938). For modern versions of the tales by far the most comprehensive and helpful list is to be found in *The Arthurian Legends: Modern Retellings of the Old Stories: An Annotated Bibliography*, compiled by Clark S. Northup and John J. Parry (*Journal of English and Germanic Philology*, XLIII, No. 2, April, 1944). A Supplement by Paul A. Brown and John J. Parry was issued in *JEGP*, XLIX, No. 2, April, 1950.

KING ARTHUR TODAY

The greatest single source of inspiration for English Arthurians has been, of course, Malory's *Morte Darthur*. Probably the most available and the soundest edition for the general reader is the one edited by Ernest Rhys for Everyman's Library (2 vols.). Of editions primarily for scholars the standard one up to recently has been the word for word reprint of Caxton's text, edited by H. O. Sommer (3 vols., D. Nutt, London, 1889–1891). In 1947, however, was published *The Works of Sir Thomas Malory*, edited by Eugène Vinaver (3 vols., Oxford: The Clarendon Press). This edition, which casts much new light both on Malory and Caxton, is a reprint of the only known manuscript of Malory's Arthurian cycle, discovered 1934 in the Fellows' Library of Winchester College.

The additional works below have been helpful in preparing the present book.

APP, AUGUST J. *Lancelot in English Literature.* Washington: Catholic University of America, 1929.

BARNARD, ELLSWORTH. *Edwin Arlington Robinson: A Critical Study.* New York: The Macmillan Co., 1952.

BEEBE, LUCIUS. *Edwin Arlington Robinson and the Arthurian Legend.* [2nd ed.] Cambridge, Mass.: privately printed, 1927.

BRODEUR, ARTHUR G. "Arthur, Dux Bellorum," *University of California Publications in English*, III, No. 7, 1939, 237–284.

BROWN, A. C. L. "Arthur's Loss of Queen and Kingdom," *Speculum*, XV, 1940, 3–11.

————. *The Origin of the Grail Legend.* Cambridge: Harvard University Press, 1943.

————. "The Round Table before Wace." [Harvard] *Studies and Notes in Philology and Literature*, VII, 1900.

CESTRE, CHARLES. *An Introduction to Edwin Arlington Robinson.* New York: The Macmillan Co., 1930.

CHAMBERS, E. K. *Arthur of Britain.* London: Sidgwick & Jackson, 1927.

COLLINGWOOD, R. G. and MYRES, J. N. L. *Roman Britain and the English Settlements.* (Vol. I in *Oxford History of England.*) Oxford: The Clarendon Press, 1936.

CROWDER, RICHARD. "E. A. Robinson's Camelot," *College English*, IX, 1947, 72–79.

————. " 'Here are the Men' ... E. A. Robinson's Male Character Types," *New England Quarterly*, XVIII, 1945, 346–367.

DAUNER, LOUISE. "The Pernicious Rib: E. A. Robinson's Concept of Feminine Character," *American Literature*, XV, 1943, 139–158.

ELIOT, T. S. "The Significance of Charles Williams," *The Listener* (British Broadcasting Corp., London), Dec. 19, 1946, pp. 894–895.

FARAL, EDMOND. *La Légende Arthurienne, Première Partie, les Plus Anciens Textes.* 3 vols. Paris: Librairie Ancienne Honoré Champion, 1929.

FISHER, LIZETTE ANDREWS. *The Mystic Vision in the Grail Legend and in The Divine Comedy.* New York: Columbia University Press, 1917.

HAGEDORN, HERMANN. *Edwin Arlington Robinson: A Biography.* New York: The Macmillan Co., 1938.

HALPERIN, MAURICE. *Le Roman de Tristan et Iseut dans la Littérature Anglo-Américaine au XIXᵉ et au XXᵉ Siècles.* Paris: Jouve et Cie., 1931.

HEIMANN, ERHARD. *Tristan und Isolde in der neuzeitlichen Literatur.* Charlottenburg: Gebrüder Hoffman, 1930.

HODGKIN, R. H. *A History of the Anglo-Saxons.* 2 vols. Oxford: The Clarendon Press, 1935.

JACKSON, KENNETH. "Once More Arthur's Battles," *Modern Philology,* XLIII, 1945, 44–57.

LOOMIS, ROGER SHERMAN. *Arthurian Tradition and Chrétien de Troyes.* New York: Columbia University Press, 1949.

—————. *Celtic Myth and Arthurian Romance.* New York: Columbia University Press, 1927.

LOTH, J. (ed.). *Les Mabinogion.* 2 vols. Paris: Fontemoing et Cie., 1913.

LOWELL, AMY. "A Bird's-Eye View of E. A. Robinson," *The Dial,* Feb. 1922.

MACCALLUM, M. W. *Tennyson's Idylls of the King and Arthurian Story from the XVIth Century,* Glasgow: J. Maclehose & Sons, 1894.

MACHEN, ARTHUR. *The Glorious Mystery.* Edited by Vincent Starrett. Chicago: Covici McGee Co., 1924.

MASEFIELD, JOHN. *In the Mill.* London: William Heinemann, 1941.

MATHEW, FR. GERVASE. A review of *Arthurian Torso* (by Charles Williams and C. S. Lewis) in *Time and Tide* (London), Jan. 1, 1949, p. 14.

MAYNADIER, HOWARD. *The Arthur of the English Poets.* Boston: Houghton Mifflin & Co., 1907.

MOORE, T. STURGE. "The Legend of Tristram and Isolt in Modern Poetry," *Criterion,* I, 1922–1923, 34–49, 171–187.

NEFF, EMERY. *Edwin Arlington Robinson.* New York: William Sloane Associates, 1948.

NITZE, WILLIAM ALBERT. "Arthurian Names: Arthur," *PMLA,* LXIV, 1949, 585–596, 1235.

—————. *Arthurian Romance and Modern Poetry and Music.* Chicago: The University of Chicago Press, 1940.

PEEBLES, ROSE JEFFRIES. *The Legend of Longinus in Ecclesiastical Tradition and in English Literature.* Baltimore: J. H. Furst Co., 1911.

POWYS, JOHN COWPER. *Autobiography.* New York: Simon & Schuster, Inc., 1934.

—————. *Obstinate Cymic.* (Includes "My Welsh Home.") Carmarthen: The Druid Press, 1947.

ROACH, WILLIAM J. "The Eucharistic Tradition in the *Perlesvaus,*" private edition distributed by the University of Chicago Libraries, reprinted from *Zeitschrift für Romanische Philologie,* LXIX, 1939.

SKENE, WILLIAM F. *The Four Ancient Books of Wales.* 2 vols. Edinburgh: Edmonston & Douglas, 1868.

SUTCLIFFE, DENHAM (ed.). *Untriangulated Stars.* Cambridge: Harvard University Press, 1947.

VAN DOREN, MARK. *Edwin Arlington Robinson.* New York: The Literary Guild of America, 1927.

VINAVER, EUGÈNE. *Malory.* Oxford: The Clarendon Press, 1929.

Vita Merlini. Translated and edited by John Jay Parry. Urbana: University of Illinois, 1925.

WAITE, ARTHUR EDWARD. *The Holy Grail: Its Legends and Symbolism.* London: Rider & Co., 1933.

WALSH, CHAD. *C. S. Lewis: Apostle to the Skeptics.* New York: The Macmillan Co., 1949.

WESTON, JESSIE L. *From Ritual to Romance.* Cambridge: The Cambridge University Press, 1920.

WILLIAMS, CHARLES, and LEWIS, C. S. *Arthurian Torso.* London: Oxford University Press, 1948.

[WILLIAMS, CHARLES.] *Essays Presented to Charles Williams.* With a memoir by C. S. Lewis. London: Oxford University Press, 1947.

WILLIAMS, CHARLES. "Malory and the Grail Legend," *Dublin Review,* No. 429, 1944, 144–153.

WINTERS, YVOR. *Edwin Arlington Robinson.* Norfolk, Conn.: New Directions Books, 1946.

II

TEXTS

READERS who wish a comprehensive list of modern texts and editions are referred to Northup and Parry's bibliography. The following list includes only those editions used in writing the present book.

ANSPACHER, LOUIS K. *Tristan and Isolde: A Tragedy.* New York: Brentano's, 1904.

ASHTON, WINIFRED. See Dane, Clemence (pseudonym).

BARING, MAURICE. *Dead Letters.* (Includes "The Camelot Jousts.") 2nd impression. London: Constable & Co., 1910.

BINYON, LAURENCE. *Arthur: A Tragedy.* London: William Heinemann, 1923.

————. *Lyric Poems.* (Includes "Recollections of Cornwall" and "Tintagel.") London: Elkin Mathews, 1894.

————. *Odes.* (Includes "The Death of Tristram.") London: The Unicorn Press, 1901.

————. *The Madness of Merlin.* Introduction by Gordon Bottomley. London: Macmillan & Co., 1947.

BISHOP, FARNHAM, and BRODEUR, ARTHUR GILCHRIST. *The Altar of the*

Legion. With illustrations by Henry Pitz. Boston: Little, Brown & Co., 1926.

BOTTOMLEY, GORDON. *Scenes and Plays.* (Includes "Merlin's Grave.") London: Constable & Co., 1929.

BRADLEY, KATHERINE HARRIS. See Field, Michael (pseudonym).

BRADLEY, WILL. *Launcelot and the Ladies.* New York: Harper & Bros., 1927.

BRIDIE, JAMES [pseudonym of OSBORNE HENRY MAVOR]. *Plays for Plain People.* (Includes "Lancelot" and "The Holy Isle.") [New ed.] London: Constable & Co., 1945.

BROOKS, BENJAMIN G. *Camelot.* Oxford: B. H. Blackwell, 1919.

BROUN, HEYWOOD. *Collected Edition of Heywood Broun.* Compiled by Heywood Hale Broun. (Includes "The Fifty First Dragon.") New York: Harcourt, Brace & Co., 1941.

BUCKLEY, REGINALD R. *Arthur of Britain. Festival Drama. I. The Birth of Arthur. II. The Round Table. III. The Holy Grail. IV. The Death of Arthur.* London: Williams & Norgate, 1914.

CABELL, JAMES BRANCH. *Jurgen: A Comedy of Justice.* [15th ed.] New York: Robert M. McBride & Co., 1924.

————. *Ladies and Gentlemen: A Parcel of Reconsiderations.* (Includes "To Sir Galahad of the Siege Perilous.") [2nd ed.] New York: Robert M. McBride & Co., 1935.

CARPENTER, RHYS. *The Tragedy of Etarre.* New York: Sturgis & Walton Co., 1912.

CARR, J. COMYNS. *Tristram and Iseult: A Drama in Four Acts.* London: Duckworth & Co., 1906.

CHASE, MARY ELLEN. *Dawn in Lyonesse.* New York: The Macmillan Co., 1938.

CHURCH, REV. ALFRED J. *The Count of the Saxon Shore: or the Villa in Vectis: A Tale of the Departure of the Romans from Britain.* New York: G. P. Putnam's Sons, 1887.

CLOSS, HANNAH. *Tristan.* London: Andrew Dakers, 1940.

COOPER, EDITH EMMA. See Field, Michael (pseudonym).

COSTAIN, THOMAS B. *The Silver Chalice.* New York: Doubleday & Co. [New issue], 1953.

DANE, CLEMENCE [pseudonym of WINIFRED ASHTON]. *The Saviors: Seven Plays on One Theme.* (Includes two Arthurian plays: "Merlin" and "The Hope of Britain." Merlin is the narrator in the others.) Garden City: Doubleday, Doran & Co., 1942.

DANIELSON, HENRY. *Arthur Machen: A Bibliography, With Notes . . . by Arthur Machen and an Introduction by Henry Savage.* London: Henry Danielson, 1923.

DAWSON, CONINGSBY. *The Road to Avalon.* London: Hodder & Stoughton, 1911.

DEEPING, WARWICK. *Love Among the Ruins.* New York: The Macmillan Co., 1904.

DEEPING, WARWICK. *The Man on the White Horse.* New York: Alfred A. Knopf, Inc., 1934.

————. *The Man Who Went Back.* London: Cassell & Co., 1940.

————. *Uther and Igraine.* [New ed.] New York: Alfred A. Knopf, Inc., 1928.

DELL, FLOYD. *King Arthur's Socks and Other Village Plays.* New York: Alfred A. Knopf, Inc., 1922.

DONALDSON, J. W. (ed.). *Arthur Pendragon of Britain.* New York: G. P. Putnam's Sons, 1943.

DOYLE, ARTHUR CONAN. *The Last Galley: Impressions and Tales.* (Includes "The Last of the Legions.") Garden City: Doubleday, Page & Co., 1911.

DUGGAN, ALFRED. *Conscience of the King.* London: Faber & Faber, 1951.

DU MAURIER, GEORGE. *A Legend of Camelot.* Illustrated by the author. London: Bradbury Agnew, 1898.

ELIOT, T. S. *The Waste Land.* 3rd printing. New York: Horace Liveright, 1928.

ERSKINE, JOHN. *Galahad: Enough of His Life to Explain His Reputation.* Indianapolis: The Bobbs-Merrill Co., Inc., 1926.

————. *Tristan and Isolde: Restoring Palamede.* Indianapolis: The Bobbs-Merrill Co., Inc., 1932.

FARADAY, W. BARNARD. *Pendragon.* London: Methuen & Co., 1930.

FIELD, MICHAEL [pseudonym of KATHERINE HARRIS BRADLEY and EDITH EMMA COOPER]. *The Accuser.* (Includes "Tristan de Léonois.") London: Sidgwick & Jackson, 1911.

————. *The Tragedy of Pardon.* London: Sidgwick & Jackson, 1911.

FRANKLAND, EDWARD. *England Growing.* (Includes as Chapter II "Medraut and Gwenhwyvar.") London: Macdonald, 1944.

————. *The Bear of Britain.* London: Macdonald, 1944.

FRENCH, ALLEN. *Sir Marrok: A Tale of the Days of King Arthur.* [New ed.] New York: The Century Co., 1914.

FRY, CHRISTOPHER. *Thor, With Angels.* Oxford: Geoffrey Cumberlege, 6th impression, 1951.

HAMILTON, LORD ERNEST. *Launcelot: A Romance of the Court of King Arthur.* London: Methuen & Co., 1926.

HARDY, THOMAS. *The Famous Tragedy of the Queen of Cornwall at Tintagel in Lyonnesse: A New Version of an Old Story Arranged as a Play for Mummers, in One Act.* London: Macmillan & Co., 1923.

HARE, AMORY [pseudonym of MRS. JAMES PEMBERTON HUTCHINSON]. *Tristram and Iseult: A Play.* With scenes [illustrations] by Wharton Esherick. Gaylordsville, Conn.: Slide Mountain Press, 1930.

HILL, GRAHAM. *Guinevere: A Tragedy in Three Acts.* London: Elkin Mathews, 1906.

HOUSMAN, CLEMENCE. *The Life of Sir Aglovale de Galis.* London: Methuen & Co., 1905.

HUTCHINSON, MRS. JAMES PEMBERTON. See Hare, Amory (pseudonym).

JOYCE, JAMES. *Finnegans Wake*. New York: The Viking Press, 1943.

KEITH, CHESTER. *Queen's Knight*. London: George Allen & Unwin, 1920.

KENDON, FRANK. *Tristram*. London: J. M. Dent & Sons, 1934.

KING, BARAGWANATH. *Arthur and Others in Cornwall*. London: Erskine Macdonald, 1925.

KINROSS, MARTHA. *Tristram and Isoult*. London: Macmillan & Co., 1913.

LEWIS, C. S. *That Hideous Strength: A Modern Fairy-Tale for Grown-Ups*. 2nd printing. New York: The Macmillan Co., 1946.

LEWIS, CHARLTON MINER. *Gawayne and the Green Knight: A Fairy Tale*. Boston and New York: Houghton, Mifflin & Co., 1904.

LINDSAY, PHILIP. *The Little Wench*. London: Ivor Nicholson & Watson, 1935.

MACHEN, ARTHUR. *Notes and Queries*. (Includes the essays "Celtic Magic" and "The Holy Grail," and the short-story "Guinevere and Lancelot.") London: Spurr & Swift, 1926.

————. "The Great Return." In *The Caerleon Edition of the Works of Arthur Machen*, Vol. 7. London: Martin Secker, 1923.

————. *The Secret Glory*. London: Martin Secker, 1922.

MARQUIS, DON. *Sonnets to a Red-Haired Lady and Famous Love Affairs*. (Includes poems on Tristram and Isolt, and Lancelot and Guinevere.) Garden City: Doubleday, Page & Co., 1922.

MASEFIELD, JOHN. *Badon Parchments*. London: William Heinemann, 1947.

————. *Midsummer Night and Other Tales in Verse*. New York: The Macmillan Co., 1928.

————. *Minnie Maylow's Story and Other Tales and Scenes*. (Includes "The Love Gift" and "Tristan's Singing.") London: William Heinemann, 1931.

————. *The Poems and Plays of John Masefield*. (Includes "The Ballad of Sir Bors.") New York: The Macmillan Co., 1918.

————. *Tristan and Isolt: A Play in Verse*. London: William Heinemann, 1927.

MASTERS, EDGAR LEE. *Songs and Satires*. (Includes "The Ballad of Launcelot and Elaine" and "The Death of Sir Launcelot.") New York: The Macmillan Co., 1916.

MAVOR, OSBORNE HENRY. See Bridie, James (pseudonym).

MITCHELL, D. M. *Sir Tristram: A Tragedy in Four Acts*. London: Fowler Wright, 1929.

MOORE, GEORGE. *Peronnik the Fool*. Mount Vernon, N. Y.: William Edwin Rudge, 1926.

MORGAN, CHARLES. *Sparkenbroke*. New York: The Macmillan Co., 1936.

ORMEROD, JAMES. *Tristram's Tomb and Other Poems*. London: Elkin Mathews & Marrot, 1928.

PADMORE, E. S. *The Death of Arthur: The Story of the Grail*. London: Herbert Jenkins, 1936.

PALLEN, CONDÉ BENOIST. *The Death of Sir Launcelot and Other Poems.* Boston: Small, Maynard & Co., 1902.

PHILIBIN, AN [pseudonym of JOHN H. POLLOCK]. *Tristram and Iseult: A Dramatic Poem.* Dublin: Talbot Press, 1924.

POLLOCK, JOHN H. See Philibin, An (pseudonym).

POWYS, JOHN COWPER. *A Glastonbury Romance.* London: John Lane, 1933.

————. *Maiden Castle.* New York: Simon & Schuster, Inc., 1936.

————. *Porius: A Romance of the Dark Ages.* London: Macdonald, 1951.

REYNOLDS, ERNEST. *Mephistopheles and the Golden Apples: A Fantastic Symphony in Seven Movements.* Cambridge: William Heffer & Sons, 1943.

————. *Tristram and Iseult.* Nottingham: John Clough & Son, 1930.

REYNOLDS, MARION LEE. *Geraint of Devon.* Boston: Sherman, French & Co., 1916.

RHYS, ERNEST. *Enid: A Lyric Play. The Music by Vincent Thomas.* London: J. M. Dent & Sons, 1908.

————. *Gwenevere: A Lyric Play. Written for Music; the Music by Vincent Thomas.* London: J. M. Dent & Sons, 1905.

————. *Lays of the Round Table and Other Lyric Romances.* London: J. M. Dent & Sons, 1905.

————. *The Leaf Burner and Other Poems.* London: J. M. Dent & Sons, 1918.

————. *The Masque of the Grail.* London: Elkin Mathews, 1908.

ROBERTS, DOROTHY JAMES. *The Enchanted Cup.* New York: Appleton-Century-Crofts, Inc., 1953.

ROBINSON, EDWIN ARLINGTON. *Collected Poems.* New York: The Macmillan Co., 1922.

————. *Lancelot.* New York: Thomas Seltzer, 1920.

————. *Merlin.* New York: The Macmillan Co., 1917.

————. *Modred: A Fragment.* New York: The Brick Row Bookshop, 1929.

————. *Tristram.* New York: The Macmillan Co., 1927.

RYAN, W. P. *King Arthur in Avalon.* London: Andrew S. Curtis, 1934.

SENIOR, DOROTHY. *The Clutch of Circumstance: or the Gates of Dawn.* London: Adam & Charles Black, 1908.

SHARPE, RUTH COLLIER. *Tristram of Lyonesse: The Story of an Immortal Love.* With illustrations from original paintings by Richard Sharpe. New York: Greenberg, 1949.

STERLING, SARA HAWKS. *A Lady of King Arthur's Court: Being a Romance of the Holy Grail.* London: Chatto & Windus, 1909.

STEYNOR, MORLEY. *Lancelot and Elaine: A Play in Five Acts.* London: George Bell & Sons, 1909.

————. *Lancelot and Guenevere: A Play in a Prologue and Four Acts.* London: George Bell & Sons, 1909.

BIBLIOGRAPHY

SYMONS, ARTHUR. *Cesare Borgia*. (Includes "Iseult of Brittany.") New York: Brentano's, 1920.
————. *Tristan and Iseult: A Play*. London: William Heinemann, 1917.
TARKINGTON, BOOTH. *Penrod*. Garden City: Doubleday, Page & Co., 1914.
TODHUNTER, JOHN. *Isolt of Ireland: A Legend in a Prologue and Three Acts*. London: J. M. Dent & Sons, 1927.
TREVELYAN, ROBERT C. *The Birth of Parsival: A Drama*. London: Longmans, Green, 1905.
VEITCH, JOHN. *Merlin and Other Poems*. Edinburgh: William Blackwood & Sons, 1889.
WARD, CHRISTOPHER. *Sir Galahad and Other Rimes: Pass-Keys to the Classics*. Illustrated by Richard Taylor. New York: Simon & Schuster, Inc., 1936.
WHITE, T. H. *The Ill-Made Knight*. With decorations by the author. New York: G. P. Putnam's Sons, 1940.
————. *The Sword in the Stone*. With decorations by the author and end papers by Robert Lawson. New York: G. P. Putnam's Sons, 1939.
————. *The Witch in the Wood*. With decorations by the author. New York: G. P. Putnam's Sons, 1939.
WILLIAMS, CHARLES. *Descent into Hell*. London: Faber & Faber, 1937.
————. *Taliessin Through Logres*. London: Oxford University Press, 1938.
————. *The Region of the Summer Stars*. London: Editions Poetry, 1944.
————. *Three Plays*. (Five Arthurian poems are interpolated.) London: Oxford University Press, 1931.
————. *War in Heaven*. [New ed.] London: Faber & Faber, 1947.
WRIGHT, S. FOWLER. *Scenes from the Morte d'Arthur*. Westminster: Merton Press, n. d. [1929].
————. *The Ballad of Elaine*. With decorations by Albert Wainwright. London: Merton Press, 1926.
————. *The Riding of Lancelot*. London: Fowler Wright, 1929.

Index

Adams, Henry, 187
Addison, Joseph, 184
Annales Cambriae, 96, 197n11, 198n20, 198n23
Anspacher, Louis, *Tristan and Isolde*, 15
App, August J., 192n24
Arnold, Matthew, 11, 15, 16, 17, 18, 74, 81, 195n32
Artorius Castus, 84–85
Ascham, Roger, 108
Aucassin and Nicolete, 11

Babcock, W. H., *Cian of the Chariots*, 196n3
Baring, Maurice, "The Camelot Jousts," 112–113
Barnard, Ellsworth, 191n2
Bédier, Joseph, *Le Roman de Tristan et Iseut*, 16, 61, 71
Belloc, Hilaire, 16
Béroul, 16, 62
Binyon, Laurence, *Arthur*, 39, "The Death of Tristram," 12, 16–18, *The Madness of Merlin*, 135–139, "Recollections of Cornwall," "Tintagel," 17
Birth of Merlin, The, 3
Bishop, Farnham, and Brodeur, Arthur Gilchrist, *The Altar of the Legion*, 85, 89–90

Bottomley, Gordon, "Merlin's Grave," 134–135
Bridie, James [Osborne Henry Mavor], "Lancelot," 192n29
Brodeur, Arthur G., "Arthur, Dux Bellorum," 198n23
Brooks, Benjamin Gilbert, *Camelot*, 41–42
Broun, Heywood, "The Fifty First Dragon," 111–112
Brown, A. C. L., 145, 197n15, "Arthur's Loss of Queen and Kingdom," 198n25
Browning, Robert, 30
Bruce, J. D., 151, 194n16, 198n22, 200n1(Ch. VI), 200n1(Ch. VII)

Cabell, James Branch, *Jurgen*, 113–114
Carr, J. Comyns, 3, *Tristram and Iseult*, 15
Case, C. M., *The Banner of the White Horse*, 196n3
Cestre, Charles, 191n2, 195n28, 196n44
Chambers, E. K., 198n22
Chase, Mary Ellen, 56, *Dawn in Lyonesse*, 68, 69
Chaucer, Geoffrey, 32
Church, Alfred J., *The Count of the Saxon Shore*, 85–86

215